PENGUIN HANDBOOKS

THE SEPARATION SURVIVAL

Helen Garlick was born in Donc... educated at Sheffield Girls' High and Bristol University, where she read law. After qualifying as a solicitor, she specialized in family law and became the matrimonial partner of a central London practice. As a member of the Solicitors' Family Law Association and a Committee member of its Training Working Party, she has lectured on the subjects of child abduction and cohabitation and in 1986 co-produced a video with the Institute of Family Therapy about conciliation, entitled *For Better or for Worse?*. She is now a freelance writer, working from home in Chiswick. She is a director of the National Council for One Parent Families, which in 1988 celebrated its 70th anniversary.

HELEN GARLICK

The Separation Survival Handbook

Penguin Books

PENGUIN BOOKS

Published by the Penguin Group
27 Wrights Lane, London W 8 5 T Z, England
Viking Penguin Inc., 40 West 23rd Street, New York, New York 10010, U S A
Penguin Books Australia Ltd, Ringwood, Victoria, Australia
Penguin Books Canada Ltd, 2801 John Street, Markham, Ontario, Canada, L 3 R 1 B 4
Penguin Books (N Z) Ltd, 182–190 Wairau Road, Auckland 10, New Zealand

Penguin Books Ltd, Registered Offices: Harmondsworth, Middlesex, England

First published 1989
10 9 8 7 6 5 4 3 2 1

Copyright © Helen Garlick, 1989
All rights reserved

Made and printed in Great Britain by
Cox and Wyman Ltd, Reading,
Filmset in Linotron Meridien by
Rowland Phototypesetting Ltd, Bury St Edmunds, Suffolk

Except in the United States of America, this book is sold subject
to the condition that it shall not, by way of trade or otherwise, be lent,
re-sold, hired out, or otherwise circulated without the
publisher's prior consent in any form of binding or cover other than
that in which it is published and without a similar condition
including this condition being imposed on the subsequent purchaser

Contents

Acknowledgements

I would like to thank the following for their individual and very special contributions towards the evolution of this book.

Mike Nathenson, for his help and feedback in developing the idea.

Margaret Robinson, for her work on children and family relationships.

Dr Judith Trowell, of the Tavistock Clinic, for her invaluable help with Chapter 7.

Diana West, for her input and continued friendship.

My parents, not least for the provision of a quiet place in which to write.

My partners at Osbornes, for their generosity and support.

Catherine, for holding the fort.

Jackie and Sammy, for giving form to the book.

My agent, Dasha Shenkman, for her astuteness and vision.

My editor, Marilyn Warnick, for her wisdom, compassion and courage.

There are many others whom I cannot name without writing another book, but who were also enormously helpful.

Finally, I want to thank my partner, Rick Howard, who is also a solicitor, for his initial inspiration for the concept of the book and thereafter for giving me the space to be able to write it as well as giving me encouragement and advice along the way.

For those who had their special parts to play in my personal experiences of separation and for A.K. and D.P. for all their individual insights and for giving me a better understanding.

Introduction

The two words 'I'm leaving' convey one of the most potent threats to the tenuous security of our existence. While the stress of coping with parting can be felt as keenly by the instigator of the separation as by the one who is left behind, it seems, at least at first, that separation most hurts those who see their partners deserting them. Their sense of personal worth can be battered to the core, and the partner left behind asks: 'Why have I failed? What did I do wrong? Why is this happening to me?' Later, however, it has to be accepted that both partners undergo very similar struggles, face very similar challenges and are fighting the same battle for survival that follows in the wake of a separation.

I am a lawyer who has specialized in family law for a number of years in a London practice. The information contained in this book is the result of my experiences with my clients who have tried to separate with dignity and create independent lives anew. The book is designed to assist you through the three interwoven processes of separation – emotional, practical and legal.

First and most immediate is the emotional reaction: anger, guilt, hurt, denial, desire for revenge – all are likely to surface in the weeks following the announcement, 'I'm leaving'. They are the forerunners of a state of acceptance of the reality of separation. Second come the practical processes: looking for an alternative home, dividing up joint bank accounts and other assets, sharing responsibility for debts, the physical aspects of splitting up. Thirdly, you may find yourself using (or being entangled in) one or more legal processes: divorce, claims for custody of the children, financial claims or applying for emergency legal relief. All of these are inter-related during the time it takes to divide one family unit into two.

The word which seems most appropriate for describing what actually happens during separation is 'journey', for it emphasizes the element of travelling, mentally and physically, from one place to another.

The book, then, is a practical, legal and emotional guide to this journey for all men and women, married and co-habiting; both those who have chosen to separate and those who have had separation thrust upon them. It is also a guide for those who are considering what might befall them at some stage in the future. Its only limitation is geographical – the legal aspects of the journey throughout the bulk of the book are confined to England and Wales, although the law relating to Scotland is outlined in Chapter 12. The law in Northern Ireland is largely the same as that in England and Wales, but there are differences in procedure and in the court structure.

At the end of the book you will find the names and addresses of organizations where you can get help.

I hope this book will aid you in mapping out your special individual journey and help you to overcome the obstacles which lie ahead.

PART ONE

THE PLANNING STAGES

1 Planning for Financial Separation

To trust is good. Not to trust is better.

Italian proverb

Everyone caught up in separation needs to start preparing for financial separation – and the sooner the better. If your partner has already departed and left you holding the financial baby, you need to start planning ahead and budgeting – you may well need to introduce draconian measures to cope on what you have. If you are thinking of separating and are planning to make a dramatic, grand gesture by walking out of the door into the sunset with your bags packed, unless you have no other options, forget it. The big wide world out there is very expensive. There are few winners in the separation process – only good losers and bad losers. The time for action on all fronts will come soon enough. Start your planning now to minimize your losses and maximize what resources you have. Take as your watchword every boy scout's motto, 'be prepared' and begin working out your own and your partner's financial positions both now and as you anticipate they will be later when you will be running separate households.

If you have to litigate your financial claims in the courts, you will find out that, broadly speaking, a common-sense, pragmatic approach prevails. The court approaches decisions to be made on the basis of 'needs and resources' – what you need and what you have got. At this point we are not looking in detail at the legal aspects or tax planning; you can check these later with your solicitor or accountant and a summary is set out on pages

105 ff. and 124 ff. respectively. Your task now is to glean as much financial information as you can about your and your partner's *resources*.

The temptation to go out on a spending spree to forget your worries may be well nigh irresistible. *Don't*. Those worries plus the extra worry of how you are going to pay for it all will come back to you with a vengeance once the spree is over. Sometimes partners deliberately and destructively go out to spend or salt away assets so that their other half can't get their hands on them. If you are married and you find out your spouse has been doing this in a big way – go immediately to a solicitor who will be able to get an injunction stopping this conduct and freezing some of the assets (see page 106). Such conduct is likely to be brought into the balance by the court at a later date and what one partner has spent in a profligate fashion or otherwise spirited away may come out of other assets which would otherwise have been assigned to him/her.

There can be no hard and fast rules about openness and trust towards your partner. You would be a fool to place all your trust in someone who has lied to you and deceived you over the years and who is apparently spending every penny he or she has – and not on you. Judge your partner fairly and squarely wherever possible. If you are still able to discuss things with one another, try to sit down together and disclose the full extent of your respective financial positions. The carrot is that you can save legal costs by coming to some sensible agreement with each other without unnecessary recourse to the courts. The stick is that if your spouse won't reveal his or her true financial position, you can get a court order for 'discovery', forcing a response to your questions and the production of documents you request. The purpose of all this is to: *get together as much financial information as possible*.

Even if you would not recognize a telephone bill if it was thrust under your nose, you *must* start gathering together as much information as you can get your hands on. Knowledge is power. Ignorance is anything but bliss. If your partner won't tell you about the financial assets, don't be afraid to rifle through a filing cabinet, desk or even a briefcase and if you can photocopy any official-looking documents inside, do so – but don't get caught. You can contact the local authority and utility companies yourself to find out the amounts of outgoings. Every hour spent on gathering information now will be worth two or three trying to sort the mess out afterwards.

Assessing Your Financial Position

There are four Schedules set out on pages 16–20 which cover: (1) Assets; (2) Liabilities; (3) Income; (4) Outgoings.

Each Schedule covers most eventualities, but if you have other items not included on the list, make provision for them. You may want to copy out these lists on separate pieces of paper three times – once for the present financial position, once for your projected position and once for your partner's projected position. On the projections you may need to make adjustments if your spouse is maintaining you or if you are paying maintenance.

Assets (see Schedule 1)

THE HOME

Who Stays Where?

If you are going to separate, you have to separate physically. It will only prolong the agony for the two of you to stay under the same roof while not sharing your lives; one of you will have to go and at least one of you is going to be unhappy about this decision. While you should never leave the home without first obtaining professional advice, examine the following factors to see which tip the scales.

1. *The children.* If you have children, your priority must be to give them as much security as possible – and to let them stay in the home with whichever of you is going to look after them. If you aim to have primary care of the children (even in the

eighties this person will usually be the children's mother) on no account should you leave the children or the home without obtaining legal advice – unless you are protecting your and their physical welfare in an emergency (see page 99 ff.). Children tend to adjust better to the fact of their parents' separation if they still have other links to steady them – their home, schools, neighbours, friends and relatives close by.

2. *Work.* If one of you works near by, the other some distance away, would it not be prudent to reorganize your home bases so that each of you can be near your work? One of you may use home as a work base, in which case he or she should usually stay there.

3. *Emotional security.* Different people react in different ways to separation. For some, to leave the home immediately following a separation from a partner may be too much to bear. If one of you needs the home to provide stability following the shock of a pending separation, it would be generous of the other to leave. Very often the partner wanting to initiate the separation *has* to go – particularly if the other denies the reality of the separation.

4. *Your alternatives.* Clearly this can be crucial. It is obviously easier to re-house one partner who plans to live alone than the other with two or three kids in tow. Can either of you lodge temporarily with a relative or friend (agree in advance how long you can stay) or obtain rented accommodation or get re-housed by the council? If you make yourself 'voluntarily homeless' (i.e. except in an emergency) and leave your home without being forced to do so, your local council has no obligation to re-house you and you may find yourself (and your children) on the streets. In these circumstances, you may both have to stick it out together until one of you gets a court order (normally within divorce proceedings) ordering one partner to leave the property or ordering a sale of the property; you can then be placed on the council's waiting list. How quickly, or rather how slowly, you are allocated a place will depend on the length of that list – some London boroughs have now closed their lists. If things look fairly hopeless where you live now, consider relocating to

another area where your chances of getting a home and maybe a job are improved.

Privately-owned Property

If you don't know already, find out:

1. *Who owns the property?* Is it in one name or held by you jointly? Is the title to your home 'registered' or 'unregistered'? The title (or deeds) to most urban and many country properties are registered at HM Land Registry. You can find out whether the title to your home is registered or unregistered by submitting an *index map search* to your local HM Land Registry office (telephone the central office to find out the relevant address).

If your title is *registered* and you own the home jointly, you can apply for office copy entries of the title to find out the name of the mortgagee. If you are not a joint owner, you will have to rely on your partner to tell you the name of the mortgagee, although you can protect your position as set out below. If the title is *unregistered*, you can search for the mortgagee at the Land Charges Department.

If you are a wife and your husband appears as the sole owner, to stop the house being sold without your consent before decree absolute, you can register a *Caution* if the title to your property is registered at the appropriate Land Registry, or a '*Class F' Charge* if the title is unregistered at the Land Charges Department (see page 174 for addresses).

If you are a co-habitee or an ex-wife and your decree absolute has already been granted and your ex-partner appears as the sole owner, you will have to start off an application to claim a share of the property before you can register a Caution or Charge. It is probably quickest to get your solicitor to take this action immediately.

If you are a joint owner of property, your partner cannot sell or mortgage without your consent.

2. *Are there any mortgages or charges secured against the property?* If so, check the name and address of the mortgagee or lender (i.e. a bank or building society) and try to find out how much is

owing. You will need to quote the mortgage account (or reference) number (printed on your mortgage statements).

3. *How much is the property itself worth?* You can phone around local estate agents on the basis that you are thinking of selling the home (you may have to!) and ask them for fair verbal valuations. Some might well try to up the price to secure a potential sale with their agency so be careful to ask for a *reasonable* price. You will need to get at least three valuations before deciding on an appropriate median figure. During periods of rapidly rising house prices, a valuation you agree now will be out of date in six months' time, so you might like to insert in Schedule 1 a provisional figure only.

When putting down the value of the home on your schedule (ignoring the mortgage) it is fairer to deduct a nominal 2 per cent of the full value to represent a notional figure for selling costs (e.g. estate agent's commission and conveyancing fees) in case one of you wants to buy the other out.

Options
1. *Transferring the home from one partner to another.* Calculate whether one of you could either transfer outright to your partner or transfer in exchange for a lump sum.

If you can afford on paper either of these options, check whether your mortgagee will agree to the remaining partner taking over sole responsibility for repayment of the mortgage. The test that mortgagees will use is whether the remaining partner has an income that, multiplied by about three, equals the amount outstanding on the original mortgage or on the original mortgage plus the top-up you will require to buy the other partner out. You could also think about taking out a separate loan to buy out one partner – but don't take on too much as your other outgoings will be very heavy. Check with your bank or building society for further information.

As another alternative you can consider a third party, perhaps a relative or friend, joining in the property with you and taking out another mortgage to buy out the departing partner's share. If you are considering this, you must take legal advice as you will probably need a Deed of Trust drawn up to declare in what shares you and the incoming partner hold the property, and you will need to make sure that your partner can't make a claim against the property at a later date.

2. *Keeping the home on.* If none of the above is feasible you could consider retaining the home until, say, the youngest child finishes school and then sell and divide the sale proceeds proportionately. Or sell in, say, five years' time. Remember, while both of you remain liable under the mortgage, the departing partner may not be able to obtain another mortgage to buy somewhere else.

3. *Selling and dividing the sale proceeds between you.* Again you need to ensure, wherever possible, that the partner who has the children has enough money allocated to buy a home for the remaining family. If the amount that remains is small and one of you intends to claim welfare benefits (see page 140), once you have more than a limited capital amount your claim for benefit will be disallowed until you have used up the balance of the capital. If you are thinking of selling and buying two alternative homes, you will probably need to synchronize the sale and purchase – which can involve phenomenal feats of organization. It is not a chain you will be dealing with but a cluster. Still, don't be disheartened – see if you can do it.

Rented Property

1. *Transferring the tenancy.* If you rent accommodation either privately or through the council, you will usually need the consent both of your landlord and of your departing partner to transfer unless you get a court order (see page 119). A landlord may only agree to transfer if he thinks the partner who remains has sufficient income. If the tenancy is in your partner's sole name, you will need to check with your solicitor if you have the right to have the tenancy transferred into your name. Cohabitees may be precluded from this.

2. *Buying somewhere new.* The prospect of buying somewhere on your own can be at once daunting and exhilarating. If you

are currently in rented accommodation, you need to prepare yourself for being a first-time buyer.* If you have children, you will still have an ongoing relationship with your partner as a parent – so it will present difficulties if you live at opposite ends of the country. Try to make sure that the alternative properties you buy or rent are within easy reach of one another if you intend to share looking after the children or if one partner intends having regular access. If one of you will be calling on your parents to help out with the children, you may need to move close to their home. Also consider the number of bedrooms – to ensure that you have room for the kids when they come to stay.

The Position for Co-habitees

As a co-habitee, you will need first to ascertain whether or not you have a share of the home in which you live. If you are a joint owner, and you and your partner have agreed to hold the property jointly, your position is comparatively straightforward. For other co-habitees, the position is not so simple. Turn to pages 127 ff. for an outline of how you can ascertain if you have an interest in the property.

If all of this sounds like a minefield – well, it is. If you have been married for only a short period of time, have no children and just one house to sell and can agree on the division of the proceeds, you may be able to do without a solicitor. Otherwise you are strongly urged to seek legal advice.

OTHER ASSETS

Bank Accounts

It is sensible to divide the bank accounts and any other accounts you hold jointly, for example building society accounts, when

* Recommended reading: *How to Buy a House or Flat* by L. E. Vickers (Penguin Books).

you separate, and open new, separate accounts – remembering to transfer any standing orders, direct credits and debits and so on. Otherwise, you may find your spouse clears the lot and the account goes into overdraft. You have joint and several liability for joint accounts – so you may be left to clear up the indebtedness even if the overdraft has been built up by your partner. If the account is already in overdraft, check with your bank manager whether you can freeze the account or change the mandate (instructions to the bank) and make it a joint signatory account so that *both* of you will have to sign cheques to make withdrawals.

The Car

To whom does the car belong and who needs it most? Argue this out between you. If you both need a car, can you sell this one and buy two smaller ones – perhaps partly with the benefit of HP (check your outgoings again to see if you can afford it)? Check the insurance policy to make sure it is valid for the other partner, if you decide to transfer.

House Contents

How you and your partner handle house contents can be a very valuable pointer to how amicable or otherwise your separation will be. Remember, they are just possessions and divide them in accordance with your relative needs at first. For wedding gifts, the usual rule is to allocate to each partner the gifts that came from his or her side of the family or his or her friends. Don't get into bitter arguments over ordinary house contents – if you end up arguing about them in court you are likely to pay three times their value in legal costs. If you possess valuable antiques jointly, you should get a proper valuation before deciding on their division, and take legal advice.

Before splitting up any other major assets, get legal and/or accounting advice. You need to check the tax implications of your various proposals (see pages 124 ff. for a brief guide) before you finalize anything.

Once you have agreed on any division, transfer the assets from the list of current assets to the projected his and her schedules.

Liabilities (see Schedule 2)

This is one area that everyone would prefer to forget about – but you do so at your peril. Take a cool clear look at your finances and then contact the relevant authorities. You must decide who will be responsible for debts and liabilities. In this context, the electricity, gas and telephone bills can count as debts, if they haven't yet been paid. Often your liabilities will have increased as, in an endeavour to buttress the failing relationship, extra demands may have been made on your bank accounts – for example to cover meals out or presents.

Don't try to pay off each debt in isolation. Work out the global picture first (see pages 117 ff. for an outline of the legal position).

THE MORTGAGE

Whoever stays in the house should be responsible for organizing mortgage repayments, even if it is the other partner who is actually funding them. If the mortgage is in joint names you both are responsible for repayment; if in one name, only the named party. Repayments should normally be made to prevent the mortgagee from foreclosing and selling the house.

THE BANK

Freeze any joint overdrafts or change to a joint signatory mandate (as above). Usually you should contact your bank manager even if he is a mystery figure to you and explain what is happening. His advice can often be most helpful. If the family finances are bound up with those of a company, check what guarantees have been given and whether the house has been used as security for a loan. If so, see your solicitor.

UTILITIES

You can arrange to pay these off in smaller lump sum payments and switch to a monthly repayment system in the future if this will help your cashflow. Don't throw away those brown envelopes unopened. Find out the worst – at least you are then prepared for it.

CREDIT CARDS

If joint, and you don't reach any alternative agreement with your partner, the cleanest thing to do is to cancel these and arrange for fresh ones in your separate names. Again, if a large amount is outstanding, write to the head office shown on the monthly statements and explain your predicament, offering to pay by stated instalments.

HIRE PURCHASE (HP)

If you have a number of items on hire purchase, consider whether you can do without the goods and cut down on your overall expenditure. The rules about whether you can break your contract with the finance company without further financial penalty are fairly complex and depend on how long you have been paying for the goods and how much you have already paid, as well as your particular contract. If you have only just bought the item on HP, you have a short period of grace under the Consumer Credit Act, during which you can change your mind. Check with your local citizens' advice bureau, giving the adviser details of your HP agreement, to see what action you can take. Most have an excellent specialist debt advice service and will not only tell you about your rights and duties, but will also assist where necessary in drafting letters to the finance houses.

BANKRUPTCY?

If, when you have totted up your assets and deducted your liabilities, you come up with a totally unmanageable figure – you and/or your partner may also be facing bankruptcy proceedings. If you see your partner facing bankruptcy, move now: as a wife you can get a court order under Section 17 of the Married Women's Property Act declaring what interest you have in the matrimonial home – which then means your share is protected against claims from your husband's creditors. As a potential bankrupt, nothing will be gained by not telling your partner. Sit down together and work out if you can handle the position financially. Seek legal advice.

Income (see Schedule 3)

EARNINGS

Although you face a massive increase in total anticipated outgoings, rarely can you compensate by boosting the income of one or both of you. Consider carefully if either you or your partner is in a position now or can place yourself in a position in the future whereby your earnings are increased. Would it be possible for one of you to go on a training course? Can you or your partner return to work? The courts can impute a 'working capacity' if it thinks one of you should be able to get a job – and reduce a wife's entitlement to maintenance proportionate to the income she could receive. If you and your partner work together, think carefully about how long that situation can remain tenable. It is often easier to go for a complete break – in work terms too – rather than hang on and watch the business deteriorate as a result of domestic strife. However, get legal advice *before* you do anything if your business affairs are inter-related. Try to think of all the possibilities before choosing your most realistic option and inserting your figures for that.

MAINTENANCE

Once you have worked out what available outgoings you will have, the higher earner (or only earner) may have to pay maintenance to the other. If you do pay or receive mainten-ance, try to get this set up on a standing order arrangement, bank to bank, to avoid potential future conflict about whether or when it will be (should have been) paid. Voluntary payments do not attract the tax relief available – you will probably need a court order. Suffice to say here that a wife is entitled to receive very roughly one-third of the joint incomes for herself with additional payments for the children. Co-habitees are not entitled to maintenance for themselves, but are for the children.

Outgoings (see Schedule 4)

Throw away any rose-tinted glasses you still have. You will never be able to survive in the future if you base your calcu-lations on false figures now. Assess first of all (this is the easy bit!) your present outgoings – as a couple or family. If you have accurate records, use the last twelve months' figures and divide these up on a monthly basis (so that you have monthly average figures which include your 'irregular payments'). This will cancel out any seasonal variations – to take obvious examples, gas and electricity bills will be much higher in the winter quarters and spending over Christmas inevitably increases. You can telephone the utilities if you don't keep old bills to check on accounts. For housekeeping, keep a running tally of the amount you spend on groceries, etc. Most people tend to be horrified by this exercise but it does at least make you realize why there is nothing left in the bank account at the end of every month. Make the figures as accurate as possible – you are likely to need several hours to prepare them to do it properly.

Now turn to the projected figures.

CAUTION

You are likely, if you are not careful, to increase your outgoings by the very reason of your being separated – for example by using a car mechanic (if your partner used to mend the car) or a book-keeper (if your partner prepared your books). The projected figures cover your outgoings in your new life – at your new home or in the existing home once your partner has left. The figures do not need to be written in stone and you may find you need to re-work them as your plans for the future become more real and you are able to gauge more accurately what the cost will be. At lot of it will be guesswork at this stage – but you can make this sensible guesswork. Now pare these outgoings to a minimum. Presents will have to be smaller or scrapped. Holidays will probably be out for a while. You will really need to economize on the shopping. You now have two sets of figures – one for yourself and one for your partner. Tot these up and compare them against your gross income. Does the sum work or do you stand to be living on credit? Re-work the figures. If you still have a loss ask yourself:

1. Can we afford to separate?
2. Can we increase our incomes?
3. How otherwise are we going to cope?

Only the two of you can provide the answers – but if you think it is tough now, think how much tougher it will be after you have separated.

Schedule 1. Assets

	Husband	Wife
Private residence current value:		
less mortgage		
less nominal selling costs		
Other real estate		
Car(s)		
Caravan		
Boat		

	Husband	Wife
Bank Accounts:		
current		
deposit		
Building Society accounts		
National Savings Certificates		
Premium Bonds		
Life Assurance Policies		
Shares in own company		
Current account in company		
Loan account in company		
Capital account in business		
Pension plan (this is a contingent interest only)		
Stocks and shares		
Interest in Trusts		
Royalties		
TOTALS	£	£

Schedule 2. Liabilities

	Husband	Wife
Mortgage on private residence		
Other mortgages		
HP debts		
Bank overdrafts		
Other loans		
Credit card balances		
Budget account balance		
TOTALS	£	£

Schedule 3. Income

	Husband	Wife
Salary, net		
Fringe benefits		

Schedule 3. Income *continued*

	Husband	Wife
Profits from self employment (less tax)		
State pension		
Occupational pensions		
Casual earnings (fees, etc.)		
Interest received:		
Bank		
Building Society		
Other		
Dividends, etc.		
Rental income		
Trust income		
Payments received under		
Deed of Covenant		
Annuities		
Other investment income		
Social Security		
Child Benefit		
Other benefits		
	£	£
ANNUAL TOTALS		
MONTHLY TOTALS	£	£

Schedule 4. Outgoings

	Husband	Wife
Regular monthly payments		
Property:		
Mortgage repayment		
Rental		
Rates		
Water rates		
Chief/ground rent		
Gas		

	Husband	Wife

Electricity
Oil
Telephone
Building insurance
Contents insurance
Repairs and decoration
Financial:
  Loan repayments
  HP payments
  Credit card payments
  Budget account
  Life Assurance premiums
  Retirement annuity premiums
  Regular savings plan
  Deed of Covenant payments
  Private medical insurance
Living expenses:
  Housekeeping
  Travel
  Clothing
  Newspapers and magazines
  Tobacco and drinks
  Cosmetics, etc.
Pets
Children:
  School fees
  School meals
  Private lessons
  Clothing
  Pocket money
  Sports
Entertainment:
  TV licence
  TV rental
  Meals out
  Family outings
  Records/books
  Sports

Schedule 4. Outgoings *continued*

	Husband	Wife
Car:		
Tax		
Insurance		
Repairs		
Petrol		
Subscriptions:		
Associations		
Clubs		
Church		
Charities		
Irregular payments		
Holidays		
Presents		
Medical/dentist		
Tax		
MONTHLY TOTALS	£	£
ANNUAL TOTALS	£	£

2 Consulting a Solicitor

Your next move, having collated all the information you can, will probably be to obtain legal advice. Neither of you is forced to instruct a solicitor. Even if your case gets to court it is open for either or both of you to be unrepresented and to act on your own behalf. However, the advantages of having a good solicitor include obtaining good, professional, independent advice tailored to your specific case. You will also make savings in time and energy as your solicitor knows the ropes – it will take you time to learn them and you may well make mistakes along the way. In addition, a good solicitor can be a support during times of crisis.

A disadvantage can be the cost, but an investment in a professional adviser's time early on to check whether you are going in the right direction may well prevent financial headaches later.

It is important to choose your solicitor carefully – and this may take a little time. A solicitor is unable for reasons of professional ethics to act for both you and your partner, on the grounds that there is or may be a potential conflict of interest between the two of you. If you have the resources to do so (remember, it is difficult to change solicitors if you have legal aid), it may be worth while arranging first interviews with two or three solicitors to ensure you get the one you want. Some people have an individual preference for a man or woman solicitor – and there are now many women practising and specializing in family law.

Self-selected sources of advice will constantly materialize. All those surrounding you suddenly seem to know someone in the throes of separation or divorce and horror stories abound. You may find yourself accosted by barrack-room lawyers', the target of unwelcome offerings of help and assistance. This is not to denigrate or deny that much-needed solace and comfort that comes from true friends. There is, however, an incalculable gulf between such support and the mish-mash of half-truths and semi-recalled tales which flood in like unsolicited mail.

Much depends on the choice of legal adviser. An inept lawyer may not help your situation at all and may indeed hinder your chances of resolving your problems satisfactorily. However, a skilled, knowledgeable lawyer with whom you establish a reasonable rapport should prove to be an invaluable guide on your path. You may be able to resolve your queries at a first general interview, but bear in mind that you may need to call on your solicitor's services more than once.

How to Find a Solicitor

If you do decide to seek legal advice at this stage, you need to contact a solicitor, not a barrister. In the UK, 'lawyer' is a generic term used to describe both solicitors and barristers. Broadly speaking, the role of solicitors is to advise members of the general public – you! – and to represent you in the lower courts while barristers provide written opinions and appear in the higher courts. Solicitors' clients are members of the public, barristers' clients are solicitors.

Your choice of solicitors depends on the area you live in and on your resources. In rural areas your choice may be between two, who in any event operate a general practice. (Have you considered travelling further afield?) In large cities, the number of solicitors prepared to take on legal aid cases is dwindling as solicitors themselves experience greater financial difficulty in keeping their practices afloat. Increasing specialization means that it is important you pick a solicitor who knows what he or she is talking about – and your family solicitor who dealt with your conveyancing or probate may not be the right person.

Personal recommendation is usually the best way of finding a solicitor. If you have limited contacts (which can be particularly the case for women at home) try contacting the secretary of the Solicitors' Family Law Association (SFLA address on page 176) for a list of members nationwide. All solicitors belonging to the SFLA must have some degree of specialization in matrimonial law and all have to subscribe to a code of practice (set out in Appendix I). Members are more likely to adopt a conciliatory rather than adversarial approach and this can achieve large savings in costs.

If you are still unable to find a solicitor, the following should provide useful contacts: your bank manager, your accountant, teachers, social workers, Citizens' Advice Bureaux or Advice Centres, or your local County Court.

Preparing for the Interview

Wherever possible, you should plan in advance for your solicitor's interview to make the best use of the time available.

It will be useful to take along with you:

1. Your schedules of assets, liabilities, income and outgoings, copied from this book.
2. A form of statement or summary. Particularly helpful if you are unreliable about dates, a summary should include: your and your partner's full correct names, address(es) and telephone number(s), occupations and ages; date and place of the marriage; full correct names of the children, their dates of birth and the schools they attend; factual details of any former marriages.
3. A checklist of questions you want to ask (see below).
4. Other documents such as your marriage certificate – if you want the solicitor to start divorce proceedings straight away.

As far as bank statements, bills and wage slips, are concerned, you need not bring anything else with you unless you are seeing your solicitor in a financial emergency (see page 106). Both of you will be able to digest only so much in the first interview – and you can always bring other documents with you later, at your solicitor's request.

The Checklist

It is wise to write down on a piece of paper questions that you want to ask the solicitor. These can include:

1. Does he/she specialize in family law?
2. What is the hourly charging rate? (This can range from £35 to £150 excluding VAT per hour.)
3. Do I qualify for legal aid? (See page 94).
4. Do I have grounds for divorce? (For married couples.)
5. What do you think will be the outcome of the case?
6. What will the cost be in broad figures?

You may find it helpful to make a particular note of what you want and don't want. Formulate wherever you can, for yourself, a summary of what you would like to achieve financially and otherwise after the separation.

Knowing what you want realistically can be more than half the battle, but if you don't want a divorce yet, for example, say so. You can confirm with your solicitor whether your wants are realistic and this can give him or her an idea about which direction to move in and how much work you want to be done. Don't be intimidated by a solicitor. With a very few notable exceptions, they behave like human beings and should respond positively to your hard work in preparation for the first meeting.

Fixed Fee Interview

Some solicitors are willing to give outline advice at an initial interview lasting for half an hour at a much reduced 'fixed fee' (currently £5). Your local CAB should be able to give you the names and addresses of neighbourhood solicitors who offer this service, although it is becoming increasingly harder to find them as the financial pressures on solicitors increase. Remember that you may qualify for legal aid (see page 94).

Maintaining a Working Relationship with your Solicitor

If the purpose of your meeting with your solicitor is simply to check that what you intend to do is fair and reasonable, your involvement with him or her will only last for one, or perhaps a couple of sessions. If, as is more likely, you need to instruct him or her to deal with your divorce and/or to bring other proceedings, he or she is likely to become an important person in your life over quite a period. You need to become organized yourself. Open a file for correspondence from your solicitor and keep copies of your own letters. Keep a separate file for all original documents and don't throw anything away before checking with your solicitor.

A plea for patience: if you cannot get hold of your solicitor immediately, remember that most reasonably successful solicitors tend to be busy – dealing with up to a hundred cases as well as yours. If a secretary tells you that your solicitor is out at court or in a meeting, this is most likely the truth and you won't help matters by taking out your frustration on the secretary. If, however, you have the ill-fortune to have landed yourself an unresponsive solicitor, try writing instead of telephoning. Give a summary of your concerns and what you would like to be done. Keep a copy for your own file. Or telephone to make an appointment and state what you want to be done. As a last resort, telephone his or her boss or the senior partner.

If all else fails, change solicitor (if you are legally aided you will have to get the consent of the local legal aid area office).

Complaints about Solicitors

If you have a real and not imagined grievance about your solicitor's conduct, telephone queries of a general nature are dealt with by the Legal Practice Information Office of the Law

Society (see page 174). Otherwise you can address your complaint in writing to the Solicitors' Complaints Bureau (see page 175). The same applies if your partner's solicitor conducts the case in an unprofessional manner. Check with your solicitor before taking such a step – which can be dramatic and may only serve to prejudice your case.

How Long Will it Take?
How Much Will it Cost?

These questions really are along the lines of, how long is a piece of string? You will have to check with your solicitor what his or her own estimates are in terms of costs and the length of time taken. Estimates of costs will vary again depending upon the amount of work (see page 92 for further details). In terms of time as a rough guideline, for an undefended divorce in London, it is likely to take approximately four to five months from start to finish, although in certain unusual circumstances you can rush through a divorce in a much shorter period. Outside London, times will vary, depending on the staffing levels and efficiency of your local court. Your solicitor should be the best person to advise you about a realistic schedule. Wherever you are situated, as you might expect, courts tend to be pushed during holiday periods, particularly around Christmas and in August, and you may well experience longer delays then. If you are forced to make financial claims against your spouse or against your co-habitee, this can take anything from one year to several years, particularly if you end up being caught in the Chancery Division as most co-habitees are.

3 Negotiation

You may feel the term 'negotiation' more relevant to super-power arms deals than to your own domestic life. Many people are actively resistant to the concept of 'haggling' over their private affairs, hoping problems will go away of their own accord. They won't. You and your partner during separation will have varying interests – some compatible, some not. You can either resolve them between yourselves, taking responsibility for the outcome, or instruct others to come to terms on your behalf. If you can, do it yourself, there are persuasive arguments for this self-help method.

There is nothing magical about the process of negotiation. Indeed, we do it every day, about whose turn it is to drive home after the party, whether to designate 'no smoking' zones at work or in the home, how much pocket money you give your children and whether this is linked to household duties, etc. The majority of us have the necessary qualities and skills within us – latent or developed – to be able to negotiate. However, to assist you in bringing those qualities and skills to the surface, the following pages give a brief analysis of the process of negotiation and give some basic answers to some basic questions such as Why? What? When? Who? Where? How? We finish by looking at the most frequently encountered pitfalls, which can trap even the most experienced of negotiators.

Why?

A gentleman in his eighties was once asked whether he was happy at having attained such a venerable age. His terse reply,

'Consider the alternative,' sums up the view you could take about embarking on a negotiation process yourself. Before I am accused by fellow-solicitors of saying that entering litigation can be likened to dying, I hasten to add that, of course, it is no such thing. There are numerous instances where the parties have no alternative but to instruct lawyers swiftly to protect their interests. However, in a vast majority of cases, couples are able between them to reach some agreements over their conflicting needs.

Negotiation is an alternative, 'self-help' method of resolving conflict. By choosing to try negotiating with your partner with a view to reaching a fair settlement, you will not only save the legal costs of protracted litigation but the process will also enable you to create an individual solution to your problems – tailor-made to suit your own particular requirements. You wrest back control over what you agree to, or don't. An added attraction can be flexibility. You as individuals can spend as long as you like in discussing your requirements and refining solutions until you both arrive at a formula which is mutually beneficial. Any appropriate agreements you make will save hours of lawyers' expensive time.

For those with children, there is an added incentive: it is absolutely essential that you recognize you can never end the relationship between yourself and your partner. You are tied together through your children, and while your relationship as husband and wife or as lovers can be terminated, that between you as parents cannot. You need to shift your focus to the parental relationship and start laying the foundation stones for positive communication in the future to enable you to deal jointly with your children's upbringing.

What?

So much is written about the process of negotiation, one could infer that it is too sophisticated for mere mortals to undertake. This is nonsense. You will already be negotiating, even if you don't realize it.

What is Negotiation?

In *Getting to Yes*,* the author describes negotiation as a 'back and forth communication designed to reach an agreement when you and the other side have some interests that are shared and others that are opposed'.

The test of what successful negotiation is all about is the goal which both parties create in their minds. Obstacles to negotiation are rarely objective but subjective – created by the negotiators themselves. If one party intends victory, someone else needs to be defeated. So how can we tell when negotiation is working and when it is not? Always keep in mind the following criteria:

1. Is it a fair compromise between each of your needs?
2. Does it enhance the relationship between you?
3. Will the terms work in practice?
4. Does it also meet the children's needs to the fullest extent possible?

To test whether your potential agreement or your proposals for agreement are a fair compromise, you need independent outside advice from someone who knows, probably your solicitor. Your solicitor can be involved in the negotiation process throughout. You should have already obtained initial advice on the merits of your case which will give you the necessary information to start negotiating for yourself. During the negotiation process, you can also keep checking back with your solicitor to see whether there are any flaws in the potential agreements.

As to whether the agreement enhances your relationship or not, consider whether you are both allowed to keep your dignity and self-respect. If any of the terms strip you of those essential qualities, they are not worthwhile.

As to whether the terms are practical, only time will tell. You may need a trial period of, say, six months to discover if the

---

* *Getting to Yes* by Fisher, Ury and Kennedy (Arrow).

arrangements you have agreed between yourself and your partner are workable.

What Can You Negotiate About?

Negotiation can be about any subject relevant to you – but be aware of the pitfalls in discussing matters relating to the children (see pages 61 ff.); you need to undertake that with special care and be responsible for what you say. Your children are dependent on you for the quality of their lives. They will not thank you in the future if you trade their needs against money. If you hear yourself or your partner starting to use the children as pawns, voice your fears. For example: 'If you unfairly reduce the maintenance, I know I will find it hard not to attempt to retaliate by asking you to see the children less. I don't think that's in anyone's interests – particularly not the kids'. Do you?'

When?

Attempt negotiation only when it is realistically possible. If your relationship has become extremely bitter and intractable, it is not really worth it. You need to reach the stage where you can distance yourself from your partner and vice versa. You must separate the relationship from the process of negotiation. You need to have gone far enough along the separation path that you can perceive your own needs objectively and those of your partner, and can communicate those needs to each other without getting enmeshed in a battle. You must be able to keep emotional distance between each other.

The specific timing can be appropriate too. It is no good launching into a weighty discussion with each other when one of you is about to go off to work or the baby is crying. Pick a time when neither of you is distracted. It is probably necessary to agree a future time in advance between you so that you can prepare yourselves.

Who?

There are two categories of people involved in negotiation, the negotiators themselves, and the people behind the scenes. The people behind the scenes can include the children and anyone else that the negotiators are involved with, as well as professional advisers.

The Children

Children, even from the age of three, can become fearful if they think they are being discussed behind their backs. You should make it clear in advance that you and your partner are discussing them, but will arrive at decisions that will be best for them.

Usually, the children should not be involved directly in the negotiation process. However, all children, particularly adolescents, have separate lives to lead and they will be unwilling to be forced into arrangements which disrupt their own plans. You will need to treat your adolescent children sensitively. If you feel there are certain stages in the negotiation that they can usefully join in, by all means allow them to do so. However, you must make it clear to the children that, while you listen to what they say, *you* have the responsibility of making the final decision. Wherever possible, you need to present a united front with your partner, so that the children do not see an opportunity to play you off against each other.

New Partners

In a way you may find yourself conducting two sets of negotiations, one with your ex-partner and one with your partner-to-be. You should make sure that your new partner knows what arrangements are being discussed. The implications of those arrangements touches on the third of the four criteria listed on page 29: Will the terms work in practice? Don't pass the buck by testing your new partner's devotion and making him or her take all the decisions. You must first of all decide for yourself what is right and then discuss it with your new partner. The unresolved business between yourself and your ex-partner is your responsibility.

Arbitrators/Conciliators

If the two of you reach deadlock over issues but none the less still wish to retain control over the outcome of negotiations, you could bring in a third party to assist in your arbitration process. If you know someone you both can trust, who would not take sides and would be able to handle your conflicts cool-headedly – that may be the person to appoint. Otherwise again reconsider the possibility of going to independent conciliation – see page 82.

Solicitors

An important behind-the-scenes party to your negotiating process is your solicitor. While you take responsibility yourself for negotiating, use your solicitor not only to obtain general advice on the type of agreement appropriate to your circumstances (which we have already discussed), but also to check specific points from time to time. Certainly you should consult him or her before finalizing anything. If you do decide later to use your solicitor to negotiate on your behalf, ensure your instructions are clear – so that he/she knows what can or cannot be agreed on your behalf. It is always a good negotiating ploy to say to your partner that before you settle any agreement, you will have to check with your solicitor. This safety-net will ensure you are not bamboozled into any prejudicial agreement and that the agreement does not have hidden flaws.

Where?

The venue you choose for conducting your negotiations will largely be dictated by your personalities (unless you are negotiating with the aid of a conciliator or through solicitors).

Restaurants or other public places can be useful to reduce the chances of your partner creating an unpleasant scene – unless he or she is likely to take advantage of the opportunity for exhibitionism, in which case choose somewhere private unless you are too hardened to get embarrassed.

Neutral ground is often a wise choice. You certainly need to find somewhere where you will not be distracted or feel claustrophobic and where you have as much time together as you need. If, however, you feel your partner will be on the defensive unless you meet on his/her home territory, be sensible and agree to meet there. The more relaxed your partner, the easier it may be to reach agreement.

A lot has been written about gaining psychological advantages over a co-negotiator by giving him/her a lower chair, making him/her face the sun, etc. It is simply not worthwhile playing this sort of game. If you feel physically uncomfortable, insist on changing the venue.

How?

The round-the-table meeting – the picture which most readily springs to mind when thinking of negotiation – is only the tip of the iceberg. Successful negotiators prepare their ground thoroughly *before* sitting down with their co-negotiators, so that they know what everyone's real needs are, what options could satisfy those needs and what their alternatives are if negotiations don't at first succeed.

There are broadly four stages in the process: (1) brainstorming; (2) creating your options; (3) meetings and discussions; (4) tying up.

Brainstorming

You need to get yourself into as creative a frame of mind as possible both before and during negotiation sessions. First, get the facts straight – leaving blanks where the outcome is uncertain. For example, when will the separation happen, who looks after the children primarily now, who lives where, how much income there is, how many debts, what other resources both human and material there are, etc. Then look at your areas of concern and the real needs of all involved – yourself, your partner and the children. For example, who will primarily take care of the children in future (keeping the relationship going with both parents), where will each of you live, how will the households be supported financially, is it possible for either to re-train to get a better job, how do you divide the house contents, who meets the HP agreements and so on. Create an exhaustive list of all your worries. The better you can understand your partner's position, the better you can answer any of his/her arguments later.

Think of these concerns as pieces of a jigsaw puzzle where, unusually, the pieces can fit together in a variety of different ways.

Now, setting aside your critical faculties, scribble down on a piece of paper all the different ways in which those concerns could be met. Be as wild and inventive as you like – suspending your powers of reason will give you options that sound crazy at first but could be adapted to fit your circumstances beautifully. If you can toss ideas around with a friend or adviser so much the better – two heads are certainly better than one.

For example, your list might run:

Re: The Home
Possibilities. Stay where I am, buy John out, move out, live with mother, live with Jill (close friend). Sell house – buy smaller flat near by, move to Cornwall, move to the States. Go on world tour for year.

Re: Care of the Children
I look after them, or John does. Or we share care 50/50. He has the children at the weekends, I have them during the week. Or I have them during the school terms, he has them all holidays except Christmas and we alternate Christmas and holidays. Visiting access – once or twice a week? At his mum's or taking them out?

Creating Your Options

From the mass of raw material generated by brainstorming, you need to discard the obviously hopeless scenarios and work with the more realistic ideas. Appraise your scribblings carefully and then start sifting the options that are most likely to work. Start moulding those into a variety of different possibilities, creating if you can a number of options which will be equally attractive to yourself and your partner. It is no good dreaming up outrageous demands or asking for nothing in the desperate hope of an agreement (see Potential Pitfalls, page 38). The options you come up with should meet as nearly as possible your and your partner's (and the kids') needs and interests.

For example, your wife has spent most of her married life looking after the children and hasn't worked outside the home for many years. The kids are leaving home in a few months. She has always dreamed of training as a beautician but hasn't had the financial resources (or, if the truth be known, your backing) to do so. It will not only boost her confidence to re-train and become self-supporting but will ensure that in the future you aren't crippled financially by maintenance payments. Instead of agreeing to pay her a low amount of maintenance to cover her needs while staying in the home (but not allowing her to do much else), work out how you could sell the house, thus releasing some capital, buy a smaller place for her near to training college and pay her fees out of the capital for a two-year course and maintenance for a fixed period of, say, four years (not to be extended) to get her on her feet. The initial capital cost may be higher but the longer-term benefits for both of you could be considerable.

To lend force to your arguments in favour of each option, you could draw on your solicitor's knowledge of what would be usual in your circumstances. If you can utilize reference to precedents (not necessarily in a strict legal sense but solutions which have a legal seal of approval) you will be bargaining from a position of greater strength.

'Working out your options' entails not only those possibilities you discuss during negotiations, but also what to do if it all goes wrong. Clarify in your mind, before you start, what your alternatives are if you can't reach agreement. To summarize, these will probably be to try again after a breathing space or another brainstorming session with your lawyer (but not if you are undertaking an up-hill battle), to appoint a third party to arbitrate, to agree to go to conciliation, or to refer the matter to your solicitor (who is likely again to negotiate on your behalf but this time from a different vantage point). Or to do nothing.

It is a good idea to work out what each of these options will cost you in practical, emotional and financial terms. You would be crazy, for example, in times of rising house prices to do nothing in the meantime if your aim is to buy out your partner's share. The eventual cost will exceed your worst expectations if you leave it for a year.

Knowledge of the other avenues which you could follow will strengthen your confidence in the negotiation process itself.

Meetings and Discussions

Your conduct during your meetings and discussions with your partner is crucial – it can make or break the success of the negotiation. If your partner has no experience in negotiation, you have more of a responsibility to take a guiding role. (Incidentally, in these circumstances, if your partner has read this chapter on negotiation it should be easier not harder to work together towards a successful conclusion.) Your approach should be to agree a settlement on the basis of what is fair to all concerned. You need to reason and be open to reason – you have to be able to put your arguments with some conviction.

A good starting point can be to outline the needs and concerns of both of you – the better you are able to explain to your partner that you understand his or her needs and concerns, the more he or she will come to appreciate you are not trying to pull a fast one. Always remember, communication is a two-way process – express your case but then sit back and listen to your partner's arguments. Letting off steam may also be part and parcel of the discussions. If this happens, listen again, acknowledge the emotions but don't get caught up in them.

In your mind, again be clear that the relationship is separate from the negotiation. Negotiating is not a point-scoring exercise but a positive method of dealing with the problems involved in physical separation.

Having laid the foundations, you can now see what issues you and your partner agree on. You might both accept, for example, that the house has to be sold, but your partner indicates that he or she won't agree to a sale going through until you have decided how much of the sale proceeds will be used to buy another house. Where you seem to run up against a problem, use lateral thinking to find ways around it. An often quoted analogy is the division of a slice of cake between two children. Both are squabbling about who should cut the cake and how much each should have. The solution? One cuts, the other chooses. This way each is assured of a fair outcome.

Lateral thinking can also include using a method or 'trick' to resolve your differences. Where, for example, you have a dispute over house contents, each of you places a coloured label on the items you want (one colour for each of you). You can then see at a glance which items are in dispute. You can draw up a list and, taking alternate turns, divide up the items between you. (If either of you is inclined to be greedy, limit the number of labels each of you has!)

Again, if you have a problem, try to find issues which you can still both agree on. If, for example, both of you have shared care of your children equally and you now dispute who should have care and control, could you work out between yourselves what access arrangements the parent not looking after the child should have? If you agree on the alternative, you increase your chances of agreeing on custody later on.

You are unlikely to be able to resolve all your differences in one go, so whenever you feel it is an appropriate time to stop – preferably on a positive note – do so. You can always arrange other dates later.

Tying up

At any stage in the negotiation process, you can check back with your solicitor for an overview of the situation. If you feel that you and your partner are reaching an agreement, consider writing it down. Putting something in writing not only concentrates the mind wonderfully on the basics of your proposals and their effects, but gives both of you more faith in each other and in the agreement itself. It is an esteem-booster. It is still, however, a good idea to head the agreement with the words 'without prejudice'. This reinforces the fact that before you agree finally on the precise terms of the settlement, you both have the opportunity to obtain legal advice on its merits. The term 'without prejudice' is used by lawyers as a negotiating device which protects any written document from being produced in court as evidence.

If, on the other hand, your negotiations have broken down without success or indeed have never got off the ground, don't feel you have failed. Some partners can behave in the most bloody-minded fashion. Now look towards your alternative options. There is much to be gained from the process of negotiation – at the very least you have learned more about your own needs and those of your partner. You have not failed.

Potential Pitfalls

The negotiation process is a tightrope; you need to take enormous care and be able to balance. There are numerous traps into which not only the unwary but also the most skilled negotiators can fall. Here are a few of the most frequently encountered.

Demanding Too Much

If your demands are too extreme, too excessive or too strident, you run the double risk of alienating your partner and forcing him/her into litigation, and of losing your partner's contribution towards your children's upbringing. It is impossible to negotiate with someone screaming blue murder. Making your partner feel guilty can have the same effect. Having checked your proposals with your solicitor, you should not fall into this trap.

Giving Up Too Much

If you are a Mr or Ms Niceguy and would rather concede anything than face a quarrel, you need to plan to avoid your overly-generous behaviour right from the start. You would only be encouraging your masochism to give everything up. To conquer your own worst nature, try the following:

1. make a list of your bottom-line requirements to enable you to start life afresh;
2. obtain independent advice (and revise your list of bottom-line requirements in the light of this if necessary);
3. while listening to alternative options from your partner, keep the list in front of you – actually or a mental picture – and never accept anything below that;
4. don't agree to anything before you have had objective advice – as a double-check.

A proviso to this general advice is 'the clean sheet syndrome'. Where a relationship has been extremely bitter and destructive, some people can feel that if they are able to generate their own income in the future and would only be able to maximize that income-earning capacity by being freed from this present relationship, the cost to them now of giving things up financially will be more than outweighed by future benefits. If you are sure you are not misleading yourself, and you have taken advice, fair enough.

Trading Children with Money

Traditionally, the balance of power is divided between the sexes so that men hold power over money, women over children. Outright trade-offs are not acceptable; moreover, they are insulting to you, your partner and the children – this is a form of blackmail. Any concession your partner is prepared to make if you bring out these weapons is unlikely to stick – people don't abide by agreements happily if they feel they have been black-mailed into them. If your partner is trying to do the dirty on you and won't listen to reason, consider either using a voluntary conciliator to shift the balance or go to your lawyer. Do not give in. Also, remember the old adage, two wrongs don't make a right. If your partner is trying to force your hand by devious methods, you will achieve nothing by lowering yourself to the same level.

Getting into a Fight

If you have a hot temper or are prone to lash out under provocation, your partner, having known you intimately, knows all the buttons to press. Don't, however, place the responsibility for forestalling a fight (verbal or physical) on to her or him. Recognize when your emotional temperature starts to rise and either cut the quarrel stone dead or get out well before you reach boiling point. Arguments are constructive only when they clear the air and between separating couples they are far more likely to be destructive. In the heat of an argument, words may be exchanged which you would never dream of uttering in your saner moments – and your partner will have the unexpected gift of future ammunition which he or she could use against you.

To summarize, the tightrope to be walked during the negotiating process is that of achieving a civilized separation between both parties who keep their self-respect intact and behave with dignity. Their aim is to create a compromise between their interests which are the closest to a fair settlement that reality can allow and, if they are parents, to lay foundation stones for a workable future relationship in which both of them can actively contribute to and be involved in their children's upbringing.

PART TWO

THE SEPARATION

---

4 Choosing the Mode of Separation

Once you have decided to go ahead with getting a separation and/or divorce, the next question you have to face is: what form should that separation take? People often insist that what they want is a 'legal separation'. Nowadays no such animal really exists, but in its place there are a variety of other species from which you can choose.

It is open to you to decide how far you are prepared to go in separating. To a great extent this has to be a joint decision with your partner. The fact that your partner may have different ideas should not deter you from endeavouring to agree with him or her the terms of separation which will make you both feel most comfortable (bearing in mind the children's needs if appropriate). Much of the agony of a separation can be attributable to the chaos of its genesis – and that agony can be relieved by the certainty of knowing where you stand and in which direction you are heading.

While long-established legal principles laid down a 'duty' for married couples to live together, in practice no court would enforce that duty and make people stay together against their will. Of the options available to you set out below, you should choose whichever is right for you at the time. For instance, it is common for couples to begin with a trial separation, then move on to an agreed separation regulated by a separation deed (often drawn up by solicitors) to last for a two-year period. This will then enable one of them to apply for a 'no-fault' divorce later, on the basis that the marriage has irretrievably broken down as evidenced by two years' separation by consent of both partners (see page 87 for details).

Look at your various choices as set out below (only the first three options are open to ex-cohabitees), and consider carefully which best meets your needs at present. Once you have worked out how the separation will be effected, you can move on to dealing with the phases covered by the next two chapters — carrying out and then coping with the separation itself.

De Facto Separation

This term is used here to cover actual physical separation. You can still be separated, both from a legal and the taxman's viewpoint, while living under the same roof but you must be leading quite separate lives — not sharing a bed, meals, washing or other household chores. If the separation is likely to be permanent, the Inland Revenue, once informed of this fact, will tax you and your spouse separately even if, pre-1991, you have been taxed together. (Under the terms of the 1988 budget, all married couples will be taxed separately from 6 April 1991.)

Trial Separation

When couples separate for a certain period this is often referred to as a trial separation. Much depends on the focus or intention of the couple during this time — is it the relationship or the separation which is on trial? If you want to keep open the possibility of a reconciliation, try to agree this in advance with your spouse, making sure, if you can, that the purpose is to improve the relationship by giving it a breathing space and letting messy emotions subside. You should also agree in advance how long it will last. The longer a period of separation, the more necessary it will be for you to come to some interim arrangements with your spouse about finances, living arrangements, access, etc.

Separation by Deed or Agreement

If the separation is likely to last, but you don't yet want to start a divorce, this tends to be a civilized method of organizing your affairs.

A deed means that the document is signed 'under seal', which can be necessary where property is being divided. A standard agreement or deed would cover the following areas:

- For you both to live separate and apart and not to interfere in each other's privacy or life.
- Who will look after the children primarily and arrangements for access to the other parent.
- Who will live in the family home.
- If the family home is to be sold, how the proceeds will be divided.
- If one party is to buy out the other, how much will be paid.
- How assets will be dealt with.
- Who pays what bills.
- Who meets legal and other expenses.

Advantages

1. Flexibility: you retain more control over the contents of the agreement – but only if you and your partner agree.

2. Often both parties can feel better about a separation agreement – they are not being pushed into a divorce and a certain degree of dignity remains intact, if the basic terms are agreed.

3. Cost: initially it can be cheaper than a divorce with various qualifications (for example, if you qualify for legal aid) if you and your partner are basically in agreement.

4. Reconciliation: it is open to you and your spouse to reconcile later and then effectively cast aside the agreement.

Disadvantages

1. Agreements are difficult to enforce if one party tries to back out of them.

2. Uncertainty: if you wish to make a clean break financially with your partner, only a court order can dismiss potential financial claims. Thus it is risky for any spouse who wants to put into effect a clean financial break.

3. Cost: some legal costs may be duplicated if you move on to get a divorce.

4. You may find that negotiations for an agreement break down or for some other reason you need the protection afforded to you by the court by instituting proceedings.

Judicial Separation or Divorce

These two have been grouped together as you need to prove the same facts to get your court decree – of either judicial separation or divorce. Judicial separation proceedings are now seldom used but may be chosen by couples who have strong religious beliefs or who need the legal protection arising from instituting proceedings but who do not accept that the marriage has finally broken down. A decree of judicial separation does not end the marriage; decree absolute in divorce does.

If you have children, you have to comply with legal processes and determine issues of custody and access (see pages 70 ff.). In many divorce courts you need not make any financial arrangements at all unless you choose to do so (although some local courts refuse to grant decree nisi until financial arrangements, at least for the children's maintenance, have been sorted out). Within the context of divorce proceedings you are able to apply for various sorts of financial relief if needed (see pages 105 ff.).

Advantages

1. Certainty: divorce proceedings can get everything sorted out once and for all – the marriage, money and the children.

2. Power: there are powerful financial remedies, where appropriate, for either spouse to apply for. In itself, this can strengthen the bargaining power of either party, particularly the wife.

3. Judicial separation decree does not finally end the marriage. This may be preferred for religious reasons.

Disadvantages

1. Cost: divorce or judicial separation proceedings can be costly if you argue with your partner before the courts. To save money it is possible to do it yourself, although this is expensive in time and you may make mistakes. Judicial separation is the same process as divorce proceedings and there may be a duplication of costs if you progress to a divorce.

2. Finality: after divorce, there really is no turning back. While there have been celebrated couples who reconcile after a divorce, you will have to re-marry if you want the marriage to continue.

3. Potential bitterness: divorce proceedings can be interpreted as a hostile step by your ex-partner, particularly as one party has to divorce the other – no joint applications are allowed.

4. Inflexibility: to an extent you have to submit yourselves to a legal process, so inevitably you lose some control over the outcome.

Which course to adopt inevitably involves you in weighing up a variety of different factors; some issues can be seen as either an advantage or a disadvantage to a particular course of action – particularly when it comes to costs. Certain problems, especially the potential bitterness and cost again, can be offset by employing a solicitor who knows what he or she is doing and adheres to the code of the Solicitors' Family Law Association.

5   The Separation Itself

Separation effects a revolution in the way we live. Many things are bound to change. Because of its radical nature, you need to know that the parting answers a real not imagined need. Assuming you have considered and rejected all other alternatives, the time has now come to approach the true beginning of your separation journey – the moment of embarkation.

If you have any choice about the point at which you and your partner separate, exercising this choice may be one of the strongest moves you can make in achieving as painless a separation as possible. The manner in which you manage actual physical separation can often set the tone for the months which lie ahead. Handled correctly, hostilities can be minimized and in many circumstances you can halt a slide into outright war.

No one can deny that separation is a difficult task. Because of this, only a fool would seek to put forward a perfect formula for achieving a perfect separation. Some separations are necessarily and unavoidably messy. If you know that you have to leave your partner but your partner is determined that he/she wants you to stay, you are both going to have a hard time. However, in all separations, even the most 'impossible', there are certain elements which go towards achieving a better than average parting. These can roughly be divided into: (1) preparation and planning; (2) communication; (3) timing; (4) commitment; (5) looking after yourself.

Preparation and Planning

A dramatic exit may provide temporary relief to your feelings, but you are laying in store a great number of problems for the longer term. The better way is to prepare not only for the moment of separation, but for what will happen afterwards (arrangements for the children, who will pay the bills, where each of you will live, etc.) to minimize the stress and confusion engendered by a separation.

It has often been said that divorce (or separation) entails not just one but a number of little divorces – not just the loss of your partner but possibly the loss of your children, your home environment, of friends; it may bring less contact with other relatives especially in-laws; perhaps a change of school for the children – you need to make ready for all of these matters. You should also prepare your partner for the separation if you can by introducing the subject well in advance and by drawing up together wherever possible your joint plans for the changes which lie ahead. It is important to prepare yourself in advance because after the separation you may well not have the energy. Separation itself makes powerful demands on you, which can have a debilitating effect.

Communication

Effective communication with your partner is an enormous boon for childless couples and essential where children are involved. This does not just mean being able to communicate your disappointments and anger to your partner but, far more importantly, being able to carve out together your arrangements for the future.

As parents you need to change the focus of your attention from that of husband/wife or of partners to that of being parents – the parental relationship is one you can never lose. By laying plans for the children well in advance, you reduce to a minimum their sense of insecurity about the future. Don't forget also to lay foundation stones for your future communication with the children – separation necessitates a change in the parental relationship too which must be accepted.

The heading 'Communication' also covers the problem of the point of separation itself. Although we may have all done it in the past, telling a partner about your intention to separate by way of letter is not the best way out. Letters or even telephone calls are second best – if you have the grace and courage and you are able to you should confront your partner face to face. If your partner is able to speak directly and openly to you in turn, the knowledge you are thereby given should also help you to behave more correctly towards him/her during the whole process. Be clear and consistent about your own intentions but let your partner speak.

Timing

There is rarely a perfect moment at which to separate but usually there does come a time which seems appropriate. You need to draw a line between excessive haste and excessive hesitation. Excessive haste usually entails the dramatic exit already mentioned – which is most likely to leave you with more problems than you foresaw. On the other hand, once you have made all your plans, you need to move and not just keep on talking about it. Be sensitive about the timing – avoid if you can times when your partner is under particular stress (for example, when ill or taking exams). Ultimately, however, the timing depends on you – and what is right for you. If you have to do it – take the plunge.

Commitment

You will need commitment to the task in hand to be able to complete it – maybe even a shade of ruthlessness. The fact is that you are unlikely to please everyone (or even anyone) about the way you deal with it. During your mission you are almost bound to experience some flak. However, if in your heart you know you are being true to yourself, strengthen your resolve and press on.

Taking Care of Yourself

This most important aspect is dealt with further in Chapter 6. Separation can be a consuming process demanding your exclusive energy and concentration. If you rarely put yourself first or you think the separation will not affect you, take particular care of yourself, otherwise you may find yourself snapping under the strain.

'Victim' of Separation?

If, against your will, you have had separation forced upon you, you may feel none of the above applies to you.

It is unbelievably hard to be the one who is left behind rather than the one who chooses to go. Added to all the hurt and anger can be the loss of self-esteem – one feels rejected, not 'good enough' for the other partner. You will need time to work through those feelings which emerge – whatever they may be. But you are not simply the victim of someone else's power. You too have the right and the responsibility to decide when to start your own process of separation – of saying goodbye to the lost relationship and rebuilding a life which supports and is good for you (an attainable goal not an unrealistic task). It is possible to keep even a dead or empty relationship going by feeding the feelings which keep you connected to your ex-partner – these can include bitterness, jealousy, vengeance. When you move beyond those feelings and accept what has happened, this is the first stage in your own creative separation process.

Separation – the Tax Man (for Married Couples)

Your local Inland Revenue office will not divine by magic that you and your partner have separated and thus need to be taxed separately. You need to inform it of this fact. Before 6 April 1991 the taxman will treat you and your spouse as separated if you are physically living apart and the separation is likely to be permanent. After 1990, married couples will be taxed separately anyway. To stop yourself from being jointly liable for your self-employed spouse's tax payments, you should advise the tax office as soon as possible. For other married people, because of the broad test employed by the Revenue, you can often choose the most tax-advantageous date as the date of separation. The information can have certain tax consequences, for example for capital gains tax exemptions if one of you leaves the matrimonial home. Check with your solicitor or accountant for details.

6   Coping with Separation

I never realized that I could experience so much pain and still live but I have learned it is a common experience.

Evelyn Waugh, Letters.

Separation is a hard journey to take – harder still for those who have begun that journey against their will. It brings us back to the raw pain of existence, uncluttered by layers of status and security. It presents a challenge to our ability to cope in the world, to our ability to achieve our individual potential.

It is impossible to predict in advance how you will cope with separation or how long it will take you to feel secure in your new life on your own. Some people never fully recover from the loss of their partner, grimly holding on to a relationship which in reality has ceased long ago. These people remain psychologically married, fearful of confronting a future alone.

How long anyone remains in this state depends largely on their past history and on their intentions. The more dependent you have been in the past on your partner, or your 'other half' to use a telling phrase, the more difficult it will be to create a new life as an independent individual. However, your intention or your willingness to overcome difficulties influence your ability to recover. If you are determined to conquer the problems, you will ultimately succeed. The greater the problem, the greater the challenge.

Frequently, the hurdles you see in front of you look unbelievably daunting – no money, no home, young children to look after, terrible feelings and fear for the future. But never give up hope. While each individual's experience is unique, the process all of us have to pass through is similar. There are ways and means of helping yourself emotionally which enable you to emerge with a life to look forward to and not be disheartened by.

People face separation in prospect with a wide variety of feelings and expectations. At one extreme, those who have chosen to leave may see it as a gateway to broader horizons, greater fulfilment, freedom, the chance to be with another person with whom they are in love. At the other, are those who never chose the path of separation but had the decision thrust upon them, those who have invested years of their lives in the now broken relationship and maybe the family it gave birth to, who view the prospect of separation with regret, bitterness, fear, even terror. Somewhere in the middle are those who know the relationship cannot continue and know it is time to move on, but view the future with a combination of sadness and excitement. Each person's experience is absolutely unique – special to his or her individual personality and circumstances. However, overall, there is a range of emotions which you are likely to encounter during the separation. These are set out on The Feelings Spectrum.

In the diagram you will find a broad spectrum of emotions likely to be experienced during the separation process. It has been structured in the form of a whirlpool, not only to represent the surges of powerful and unfamiliar feelings which rush through you but also because each person will experience a different combination of various emotions. Change has a re-volutionary effect upon us all and there are many stages each person has to go through before attaining what is perhaps the mark of the end of the separation process – true acceptance of the situation and forgiveness of one's partner.

Before you reach that goal you have to experience fully all the earlier stages, whether they be denial, anger, grief or exhilaration. Allow the emotions to wash through you without trying to suppress them. Such suppression will only in itself delay the healing process.

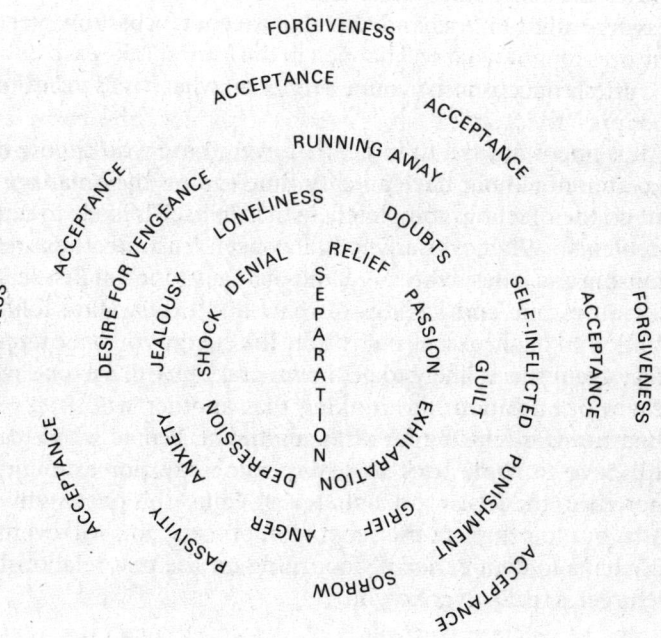

The length of time it will take to journey through each stage towards an acceptance of the separation is again variable. As a rough rule of thumb I would say two years, but it can be more or less depending on each individual. Turn your focus, however, to the present not what will happen in the future. Take each day as it comes, concentrating your energies on what needs to be done today.

It is important not to forget that even those who choose the separation will not have an easy time (unless they manage to cut off their feelings completely, which in itself is likely to cause problems). Whenever anybody has been frustrated by a relationship and is desperate to get out of it, separation at first seems like an escape and feelings of relief and exhilaration follow. While you might as well enjoy fully the energy you have tapped into, again this is likely to be a temporary phase. Anyone who leaves one relationship thinking that another will supply all their needs is heading for disappointment. People who escape still have to come back to reality some day (for example, a mortgage, children, work, whatever). Enjoy this phase while it lasts, but to complete the separation process, you will eventually have to do a period of mourning for the past relationship before it is really over for you.

Confronting Your Fears

In a sense, all of the emotions viewed as 'negative' stem from or are closely linked to fear. The fear of being alone is particularly prevalent among people who have never lived on their own and who have no interests outside the family. Fear of and resistance to change and the underlying fear of never being able to find anyone else are potent fears. As with all fears, the only effective way of dealing with them is to confront them head on, within the limits you feel you can cope with for the time being.

Face your fears squarely and recognize them for what they are – spectres manufactured by your imagination. Have a few test runs at first. Try spending more time on your own and take up a hobby which will give you some interest for the future.

Have friends to stay over at the weekends initially if this helps. Allow change to happen. Allow yourself, when the time is right, to be open to other relationships. Consider the worst that could possibly happen – work out how you would deal with that eventuality and then go ahead and see what reality brings. As you expose these ghostly fears to the light of ordinary existence, they will disappear.

Looking After Yourself

Your first and most important relationship is the one with yourself. Be a friend to yourself and treat yourself kindly, as you would any other person in need. Sometimes, with work commitments and/or children to look after, it is not easy to take time for yourself. The chances are that the separation itself will seem to drain you of energy. It is none the less of the utmost importance to take care of yourself first, even if you have only half an hour to yourself each day. You will not be able to look after other people or fulfil your work obligations if you are exhausted. Tiredness and lack of energy are natural bodily reactions. All you need to do to get over them is take time and give in to them. Sleep. Play soothing music. Take long, hot baths. Particularly if you live surrounded by others, create one place as a safe haven for yourself – whether it be your bedroom, a special corner of the garden or even the bathroom. In that space ensure you can cut off from the outside world and just relax.

Body and mind are inseparably linked. To look after your body is to look after your inner self. Make sure that you eat properly according to your needs. Do get lots of rest. Take plenty of exercise – exhausting yourself physically can be a great relief. It will enable you to sleep more soundly and you will feel better about yourself. Try to take vigorous exercise, say an hour's walk or half an hour's swimming or jogging, at least three times a week.

The temptation after separation is to abuse your body and escape from the pain of reality through alcohol or drugs such as tranquillizers. No one will deny that the occasional drink can help you to relax; on the other hand, hitting the bottle hard or abusing drugs and hence your body will only postpone dealing with your problems. Far better to face your feelings today and begin the healing process.

Talking It Out

With Friends and Relations

Separation marks a time when you find out who your true friends are. Sometimes, put to the test, people you previously thought of as good friends fail to come up to scratch. You may have some 'dead wood' to cut away in terms of outdated relationships. People also tend to express opinions based on their own experiences and prejudices. Thus, married people can urge you to greater endeavours towards reconciliation which no sane person would contemplate. Divorcees can be anxious to extol the virtues of divorce and even become evangelistic in their attitudes.

The best of friends are those who simply listen and are there for you; allowing you to express your feelings (anger, sadness, nostalgia, maybe even the odd tear or two). Such friends give you room to be yourself but can tell you when you are going too far or over-indulging yourself. Cultivate and cherish such people. If you have one or two in your life, you are blessed.

Relatives present a more complex picture – after all, unlike friends, you didn't chose them. Relatives can be your staunchest of allies or they can try to push you into a position you do not want to be in. Again, all you can do is be true to yourself. If you find relatives or friends make you feel depressed and are not helping *you*, tell them gently but firmly that you would prefer to be on your own.

Counselling and Therapy

Do not feel a failure if you contemplate seeing a counsellor or therapist. On the contrary, it is a courageous step to take to help you through this time and, as a bonus, you are likely to get to know yourself a lot better.

Therapists charge upwards of £10 per session and will normally arrange meetings on a weekly or bi-weekly basis for 'as long as it takes'. To have the full benefit of therapy, the commitment is likely to be long-term but you may choose to undergo therapy for, say, a trial period of three months. How beneficial the therapy is depends on the quality of your therapist. Many therapists work in groups or associations and, after an initial interview to find out your needs, you will be recommended to a particular therapist with whom you make your own arrangements. While at first glance the cost seems high, it is a better investment than drink, drugs or any other expensive escape mechanisms.

HOW TO CONTACT A THERAPIST

The numbers of therapists practising throughout the country are unevenly spread. In London, if you can afford to pay privately, you have freedom of choice. Elsewhere there may only be one therapist for a large catchment area.

Try your local Marriage Guidance Council (now called Relate) – who work with co-habiting couples and single people where appropriate – for work on your relationship.

For individual counselling, ask your friends or colleagues for names of therapists or groups of therapists whom they would be prepared to recommend.

Alternatively, your GP may be able to refer you to a local clinic or independent therapist (your fees may be payable by the NHS if your problems are severe).

PART THREE

THE CHILDREN

Children are at the core of decisions relating to separation and divorce, and in recognition of this I have placed this section at the heart of the book. At the same time I have deliberately dealt with the subject of children separately, so that you can skip it if it does not apply in your case.

7   Children's Feelings and Behaviour

The effects of most crises, including divorce and separation, will wane over time. Children are flexible enough to adapt, although they may not do so willingly at first. The success of their adjustment depends on the quality of the child's relationship with *both* parents, the child-caring practice of the custodial parent and the availability of support. Children who find themselves in a stable, conflict-free situation will usually recover within, say, a two-year period from the hostility and tensions associated with separation and divorce. The eventual outcome depends not only on what has been lost but also on what has been created to take its place.

Many problems that parents have over the children are most prevalent at the beginning, just after the separation has occurred. A common reaction for parents early on is concern over the fact that their children seem sad either before or after an access visit. In fact, when their parents have just separated, sadness is *more* normal than no exhibited signs of distress – the children are going through their own grieving process for the end of their parents' relationship. Also, non-custodial parents should be wary of 'goody goody' behaviour during access visits. It is important for a child to be able to spend sufficient time with the non-custodial parent precisely so that he or she can behave 'normally' – i.e. expressing anger or distress, or being able to do the various mischievous things that children get up to. Encouragement of longer access periods for fathers is not purely altruistic for mothers – research suggests that fathers who see their children regularly tend to be more regular in their maintenance payments. Longer term, a custodial parent having to look after the children day in and day out would probably welcome the break afforded by the non-custodial parent looking after them for a while.

This chapter outlines the way children may behave during the separation process, starting off with a bird's-eye view of child development. It offers guidelines on how best to manage the children during this difficult time. Chapter 8 explains the different legal processes you may be involved in.

How Do We Recognize Our Children's Feelings?

In the turmoil of our own pain and suffering, it is often hard to recognize the traumas suffered by our children. This can be compounded by guilt – hating to think we are responsible for their unhappiness. It is often easier to pretend the children are OK, refusing to acknowledge that they have their own divorce or series of separations (e.g. saying goodbye to dad, leaving a school, leaving the family home, leaving friends) to go through. Even if we are able to look up from our own misery, it can be difficult to understand what the children are feeling. They can be unpredictable in their reactions and in what they say and do. How can we distinguish whether or not they are coping with their own personal crises? How can we tell if we need to seek outside help?

The first thing is to realize that children are not miniature adults and their behaviour and reactions cannot be understood by comparing them with typical adult behaviour and reactions. You know your child better than anyone else. However, the very closeness and intensity of that relationship may make it difficult to step back and look objectively at how your child is behaving. Children have their own ways of behaving appropriate to their age and development. So set aside your preconceived ideas and try to get under the child's skin – 'to walk two moons in his moccasins' to borrow an apt, if odd, Red Indian phrase. This is no easy task, but essential if you are to grasp how the separation is affecting the children.

How are Children Likely to React?

How do differently-aged children react to separation and divorce? It may come as an unpleasant surprise to learn that recent research shows that nearly all children want their parents to stay together, however bitter and painful the parental relationship. In the past it was generally conceded that it was better for the family if hostile parents broke up, alleviating the tense and angry atmosphere of the home. Children usually disagree with this and are likely to dream of their parents' reconciliation years after the separation. Older children may be sufficiently mature to recognize their parents' need to separate, but their younger siblings will still be hoping against hope that Mum and Dad will get back together. Parents find that their children will go to great lengths to try and effect a reconciliation.

Other strong emotions which tend to affect children of all ages are fear of abandonment and anguish at their own powerlessness. If one parent leaves, they are terrified the other will leave too. This fear can be displayed in a variety of different ways, from behaving in a 'clingy' fashion to pretending not to care at all, but becoming very angry if the parent looking after them wants to go out for the evening. Also it should be borne in mind, to state the obvious, that children do not, as a rule, choose that their parents should separate. They often feel extremely angry at their own powerlessness, not only about the separation itself but also about what arrangements are being made for their future. As a rule, children have little or no say in the legal process concerning what will happen to them.

In terms of specific age groups, *up to six months*, a baby is unable to distinguish other people from himself. Baby is the centre of the universe. In fact, he or she (to him or her) *is* the universe. He or she does not realize that parents are beings existing in their own right. Baby is utterly dependent, of course, upon his or her primary caretaker and it is a matter of life and death whether the parents are able to keep one end fed and watered and the other clean and dry. However, before six months, *who* actually performs this crucial role may not matter so much, as long as *someone* caring is there. Baby also will be aware only in the very vaguest of ways if anyone other than mother is in the household. Thus, before the baby's attachment to other figures forms, it is a better time to separate before the child reaches six months.

Thereafter, the period from *six months to three years* is often classified as the most crucial period in any person's life. The disruption involved in a separation may well have a profound effect on children in this age band. It can often be difficult to explain to pre-school children what is happening. Their thinking is very different from that of adults. Almost certainly they will think they are the cause of the separation and will thus feel in some way responsible for the break-up. Children at this age frequently take refuge in 'magical' thinking — believing that if they think something hard enough it will really come true. They hope and think their parents will get back together again — if their 'magical' wishes then don't work, the burden can be doubly hard for them to bear. Outwardly, they may appear to react less than older children — indeed, to be almost unaffected. The truth is more likely that they refuse to allow themselves to accept what is happening because it is too painful for them.

Between the ages of six and ten, children come to realize they are no longer omnipotent. This age is an in-between stage and is always hard to bear. Younger children (six to seven and a half) will tend to react towards separation by going backwards — retreating into the magical thinking and denial commonly associated with pre-school children. From nine and a half upwards, children may react more like their stormy adolescent siblings. While both type of reactions have their attendant problems, these children are at least coping in their own way. A particularly vulnerable age group are the ones caught in the middle (the seven-and-a-half to nine-and-a-half-year-olds). They are too old to retreat backwards and block off their feelings, too young to get rid of their feelings by being able to express them in words and actions. These children can withdraw, become depressed and have learning difficulties at school.

In *adolescence*, children are more likely to react in an extreme fashion – retreating into their own world or becoming uncomfortably articulate and explosive in their anger. While the latter reaction is more unpleasant to witness, these children are coping better through their ability to shout out their angry feelings – they are less likely to suffer later. Those who become very quiet are likely to be suffering inside more. Adolescents in whatever situation have to go through their own personal crises of identity and of sexuality. Parental separation will create even more of a challenge to these newly blossoming individuals. They are particularly sensitive in terms of their own sexuality and they may become over-jealous of other parental relationships or start to step up their own sexual experiments and throw themselves into sexual encounters. At school, too, they can either lose themselves by extensive involvement in their work or lose all interest in it and fall behind.

It is important also not to forget *older adolescents* (up to twenty-one years) who are still living at home, or returning home during vacations. For students particularly, a major crisis can arise when their parents divorce – not least in terms of practicalities. Where will they go in the holidays? Where will they spend Christmas? Do not ignore the feelings of your 'young adult' children; give them clear guidelines about what will happen in the future.

There are certain advantages in dealing with adolescents involved in separation. Adolescence is a time when children effectively give their parents a second chance to put straight problems that have occurred in the past. While difficult and temperamental, adolescents are more open to working on their feelings and problems. Adolescence can be an enormously valuable stage in which parents and children can come to a new and better understanding.

Guidelines on Dealing with Children During Separation

The awareness that your children will suffer in separation can be depressing. It is far easier to ignore children's suffering than to recognize it for what it is. In the past, children in divorcing families were largely overlooked and subsequent studies have shown that their mental health and later performance were badly affected. Long term, it is far better to realize that children also have a role to play in separation and to plan in advance how best to deal with them and to minimize their pain.

What could be termed 'post-separation behaviour' will always take time to work through – but should usually begin to resolve itself after six months to a year. If after that time your child is still exhibiting overt or covert signs of distress, or if at any time the child is behaving unmanageably or at the extreme end of the ranges outlined above, do consider contacting outside help. Some addresses are included in the list on pages 172 ff. If these are inconvenient, a method of tracking down help is detailed on page 68.

Given all this information, how can you as parents best manage your children during divorce and separation? Below you will find guidelines on the best you can do. This approach is emphasized because you can do no more than your best. Feeling guilty and blaming yourself are negative, destructive emotions. Set them aside and get on with the task of concentrating your energy on your and your children's successful survival in this process.

1. Give your children accurate information about the separation and explain it to them, gently, in a way appropriate to their ages.
2. Don't hold out false hopes of a reconciliation. The sooner the children know the truth, the easier it is to come to terms with it.
3. Arrange regular access to the parent who doesn't have primary care. Longer periods of access when children stay over with the other parent are more beneficial than short, uncomfortable visits.
4. Work together with your partner and be consistent in your approaches towards the children. Tell them jointly, if you can, about the separation. Don't let them play you off one against the other.

5. Turn the focus of your relationship with each other to-
    wards the parental role, leaving behind you the discarded
    husband/wife relationship.
6. Minimize the 'secondary' divorces. Encourage the chil-
    dren to maintain their links with friends and relatives
    (particularly grandparents). Keep on the family home if
    you can to build up their sense of security.
7. Affirm frequently your continuing love for the children
    and assure them they are in no way to blame for the
    break-up.
8. Be responsible about telling others to minimize the
    embarrassment your children might otherwise have to
    overcome. For example, think of contacting other rela-
    tives, their schools, and their friends' parents. Telling
    others early on has the added benefit that they can then
    understand better any unusual behaviour on your chil-
    dren's part. This also frees the children to talk to others if
    they want to.
9. Allow, and encourage when you can, your children to
    share their experiences with others of their own age and
    talk privately to someone independent.
10. Allow time to pass. Your children's sense of security will
    need time to become established.

The key to 'the best you can do' is twofold – communication
and regular contact. Research has shown that the more access
the children have with *both* parents, particularly in the period
just after separation, the better able they are to adjust. Communication is vital – both with the other parent and with the
children.

Telling the Children about the Separation

Telling the children can be one of the most difficult moments of
all separation – so painful in prospect that many parents pro-
crastinate and can't bring themselves to talk to the children at
all. However, informing the children in such a way that they can
understand what you are saying, reassuring them they are not

to blame, ensuring that both parents continue their love and support and giving them a chance to talk through their fears and feelings are all crucial in helping the children to adjust.

Where to Find Therapeutic Help for Children

There is no single body or national head office to which one can turn for help. There is no comprehensive directory of specialists throughout the country. Do not be deterred.

1. Turn first to your local telephone directory and look under Health, Education or Social Services for your local child and family psychiatric clinic, child guidance clinic, child psychological service or other similar provision.
2. If you have difficulty, consult your local Citizens' Advice Bureau which should be able to help.
3. If all else fails contact your local school (or, if the children are of school age, the children's own school). They will be able to refer you to their school psychologist. Every school is required by statute to have one. The school psychologist should be able to refer you to the appropriate local resource centre.

Access

DOS AND DON'TS

For custodial parents: actively encourage access, including staying access, right from the beginning. You will be helping the children enormously. You may appreciate the benefits, longer term, of having some time for yourself.

For non-custodial parents: don't 'disappear' and avoid access visits because they are so painful. If the pain initially involved is faced head on at an early stage, it will diminish over time.

Always leave a contact telephone number and address for the custodial parent where access involves an overnight stay.

For both parents: don't denigrate the other parent when talking to the children.

Don't trade kids with money.

Do make the beginnings and endings of access as smooth and trouble-free as possible. Be punctual. Get the kids ready on time (with overnight bags if necessary). Don't leave the custodial parent at the end of an access period with a load of dirty washing.

Agree access plans in advance wherever possible – if there has to be a change make sure the other parent and the children are told as soon as possible.

Show mutual respect for the other parent's privacy and don't use the children as go-betweens. Speak to the other parent direct about any queries.

Be sensitive about either of you bringing along a new partner. Remember, the children need quality time spent alone with their parents and will need to be introduced gradually to any new partner or even potential step-parent.

Arrange longer access visits in the holidays – the longer the period of access the better.

THE ACCESS CALENDAR

Children can often find themselves confused about when they are to see the other parent. A good way of dealing with this can be to give each child an 'access calendar' (any calendar which shows a year on one sheet will do) marking it with, for example, stars when the child is going to see the other parent. You can also put on different coloured stars for important events like birthdays, outings or treats. The access calendar can be planned in advance with both parents then afterwards is a continual visual reminder to the children about when they will next be seeing Daddy or Mummy.

8 Legal Concepts and Applications

Whatever your arrangements for the children as *divorcing* parents, these will have to be translated into legal concepts. In 1986, the Law Commission recommended that no court orders be made on divorce relating to custody of the children, save in particularly problematic cases. After all, why should divorcing parents be distinguished from their still married counterparts? However, that radical proposal is not yet the law and, until law has been changed, there are various legal categories which you have to fit into and court orders which have to be made.

Court Orders

Custody

Means: the bundles of rights and responsibilities parents have towards their children. The right and duty to take major decisions concerning their upbringing (although the parent having 'sole custody' should still consult the other parent).

You can apply for: *sole custody* (for one parent) or *joint custody* (for both).

Effect: joint custody is the nearest court order you can get resembling the pre-divorce parental role towards the children. In a sense, the effect of a joint custody order is primarily psychological, as both parents feel they have a recognized role to play towards their children. Orders for joint custody are becoming more common as the importance of the paternal contribution becomes more accepted.

Care and Control

Means: actual physical 'possession' of the child.

You can apply for: *sole care and control* only, not joint.

Effect: care and control is what most laymen mean when they talk about custody. The courts will not split care and control, the current view being that the child must know where his or her first *home* is.

Confusingly, people talk of the 'custodial parent' as the parent who has care and control of the children and the 'non-custodial parent' as the other parent. Other terms used are 'the person having primary care' or 'caring parent' and the 'non-caring parent'. None of the terms coined is particularly apposite and some are downright insensitive to the role of the father (who is usually the one not looking after the children most of the time). Throughout this book the terms 'non-custodial' and 'custodial' parent will be used.

Access

Means: visitation periods for the parent not having care and control. Can be 'staying' or 'visiting' access.

You can apply for: *reasonable access* or *defined access*.

Effect: 'reasonable' (or, rarely, 'generous') access is a flexible order made where the parents can agree on arrangements between themselves. With 'defined' access, visiting or staying access periods are fixed in advance, sometimes down to the precise hour of collection and return of the children. Defined access can also cover important recurring dates in the child's calendar, for example Christmas, birthdays and holidays.

The Section 41 Appointment (for divorcing parents)

If divorce proceedings have commenced, in the divorce petition you have to include a statement as to whether or not there are any 'children of the family' (children of both parents under sixteen or under eighteen and attending full-time education, or other children treated as members of your family). A statement of arrangements for the children must be lodged with the petition, summarizing where they are to live, attend school (if appropriate) and what maintenance (if any) has been agreed.

Occasionally, parents may disagree over whether either partner's children count as 'children of the family'. However, unless the marriage has been very short and a family unit was never created of the different members, children will always be designated children of the family.

Wherever there are children of the family, the court sets aside a separate children's appointment before the judge, normally on the date of decree nisi. It is necessary for the custodial parent to attend personally, but it is a good idea for *both* parents to attend to answer any of the judge's queries. The hearing (called the Section 41 Appointment) is comparatively informal and lawyers seldom attend. It is the judge's duty at the Section 41 Appointment to ascertain that the arrangements made for the children are *'satisfactory'* or *'the best that can be devised in the circumstances'* and a Section 41 certificate is then given. This declares how many children of the family, as defined above, there are, their names and dates of birth, it makes orders for the custody, care and control and access and states whether the judge approves the arrangements. Without such a certificate you will be unable to perfect the divorce later and obtain decree absolute. If you are in any disagreement about the children over any issue of custody or access, the Section 41 Appointment will normally be adjourned and you then need to consider what step to take next.

Battles over the Children

On page 74 you will find a flowchart summarizing the steps that make up a contested claim for custody (sole or joint), care and control (sole) or access (reasonable or defined). Such cases are always heard by a judge, not a registrar (unless you are involved, outside divorce proceedings, with magistrates' courts). Only 6 per cent of divorces involving children involve a *contest* over the children. The flowchart emphasizes that you can step off the bandwagon whenever you want by coming to an agreement with your partner. Most parents agree between themselves and often settlements are made on the steps of the court. This is not surprising as fights over children are very painful to all concerned, not least the children. All too often, the courts have to choose between two parents who are equally matched and who would be equally well able to fulfil the task of custodial parent. Judges face an impossible task where the ultimate decision cannot be 'right'. Custody battles can here be more of a lottery than anything else. With other families it will be clear, to outsiders at least, who would be the 'better' parent to look after the children full-time, but the other parent still drags on with a battle over who will have custody. The motivation can be complex – maybe to hurt the other parent or prove to themselves that they really do care about the family.

Conciliation Appointments

If either parent makes an application to the court about custody or access, the first stage is for the court to fix a conciliation appointment. Both parents are asked to attend, together with children over a certain age (usually about ten) and sometimes their legal representatives. The divorce court registrar sits with a court welfare officer and both try to work out with the parents an arrangement which would suit them. If no agreement is reached, the registrar will make an order for directions of the case which will fix, for example, when each side should file affidavits and the case is then set in motion for a full hearing. No nationwide figures are available but it is estimated that agreement is reached in about 20 per cent of all cases at the conciliation appointment and many more cases settle before trial.

Court Considerations in Battles over the Children

1. THE WELFARE PRINCIPLE

The court always tries to look at the conflicting parental claims from the child's viewpoint. 'The welfare of the child is of first

Flowchart for Contested Custody/Access Proceedings

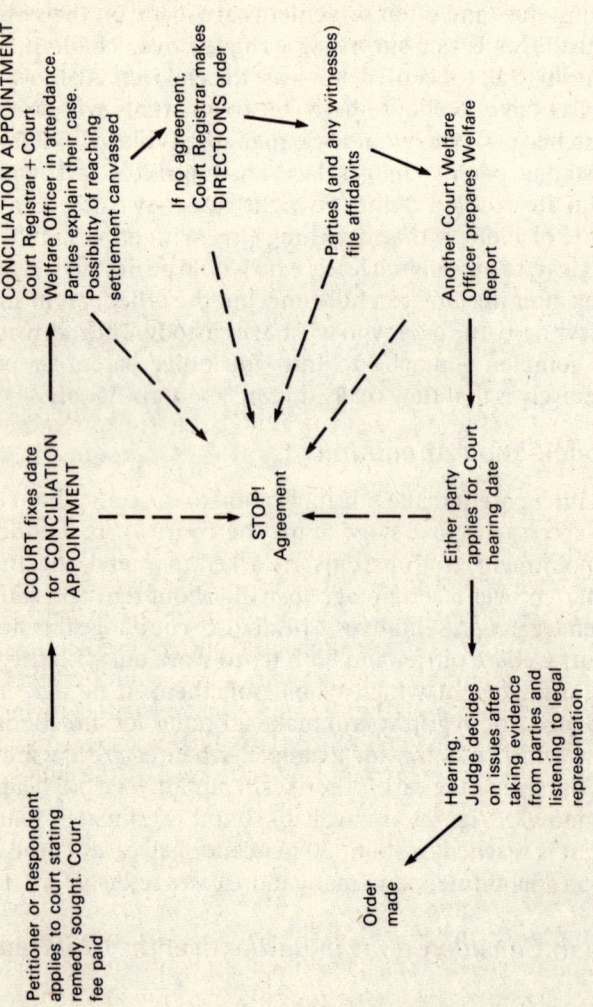

Petitioner or Respondent applies to court stating remedy sought. Court fee paid

COURT fixes date for CONCILIATION APPOINTMENT

CONCILIATION APPOINTMENT
Court Registrar + Court Welfare Officer in attendance. Parties explain their case. Possibility of reaching settlement canvassed

If no agreement, Court Registrar makes DIRECTIONS order

Parties (and any witnesses) file affidavits

Another Court Welfare Officer prepares Welfare Report

STOP! Agreement

Either party applies for Court hearing date

Hearing. Judge decides on issues after taking evidence from parties and listening to legal representation

Order made

and paramount importance' is a phrase etched on every family lawyer's mind. It is hard to define the welfare principle in any detail. Suffice to say that the court tries to evaluate which outcome would be in the best interests of the child. In earlier days it was very difficult for the court to weigh up the strength of each party's claim. Now, in all cases a court welfare officer is instructed to prepare a report which gives the court an independent viewpoint and explains the background of the case. The welfare officer's report usually weighs heavily with the court and if a recommendation is included, a judge is unlikely to deviate from it.

2.   THE STATUS QUO

Courts are most reluctant to make children undergo any further changes on top of those which they have already experienced. If the children have established a pattern or routine in terms of where they live and with whom, which provides them with the love, security and support they need, the court will be reluctant to upset this. If you are proposing a custody change to the court, you must act quickly – time is always against you.

On the other hand, over issues of access in particular, the court will not sanction the status quo where it is against the child's best interests, for example, where a mother is refusing to give access to the father because she feels bitter towards him. Access is seen as the child's right and whenever possible the courts will lean in favour of access to keep up the child's contact with *both* parents.

3.   HOMOSEXUALITY AND THE LAW

In the past, a number of cases have gone against lesbian mothers claiming custody of their children, particularly where the mother is co-habiting with her lesbian lover. The question of sexual preference can be a determining factor, although the courts should look primarily at the quality of care offered by each parent. The issues are complex and cannot be examined in depth here. If you are facing such a situation, you need to obtain expert advice from a lawyer who is experienced in this area: try contacting Women's Aid (see page 176). There is also an excellent handbook specifically on this subject: *Lesbian Mother's Legal Handbook*, a Rights of Women Lesbian Custody Group book (Women's Press Handbook Series).

4.   ANY OTHER CONSIDERATIONS

Apart from formulating the welfare principle and tending to make decisions which confirm the status quo, courts have been reluctant to give any hard-and-fast rules in order to preserve their flexibility in being able to judge each case on its merits. Obviously, other factors are taken into consideration but the courts don't like putting these down in black and white. The approach is thus flexible, but makes prospects rather uncertain for parents facing battles over their children. In 1986 the Law Commission published, as part of a Green Paper on Child Custody, a draft checklist which is reproduced as Appendix II on pages 160–61. Again, you should remember that this list does not form part of the law and can only be seen as a rough guide. The problem remains that in any case one major consideration may outweigh all the others and however many minor 'points' you may tot up, that major factor may be against you.

5.   DO THE CHILDREN HAVE ANY SAY?

The court welfare officer preparing the report should interview the children to find out what they want. Hard-working welfare officers (bearing in mind that because of limited numbers they are not always able to make all the investigations they would like) may speak to the children's schools and anyone else who has had family involvement, such as a social worker. On rare occasions, the judge may ask older children (over about ten) to go to court to talk to him or her in private.

As children get older, they effectively vote with their feet, namely they will go and live with the parent they want to be with.

What Happens if You Don't Like the Court's Decision?

The answer is, in 99 cases out of 100: tough. The courts are hard indeed on parents who lose at first instance. Following a recent case, you have to show that the judge at the hearing was 'plainly wrong', a test even harder to satisfy than to prove that the appeal court itself would have come to a different decision. The appeal court has not infrequently stated that while it might decide differently, it will refuse to overturn the trial judge's ruling.

The Children and Money

For Spouses

Once divorce proceedings have started, you can apply for maintenance (which can include an order for a school fees payment), a *capital sum* or *property adjustment* (see page 120 for a fuller explanation). You will need to give evidence of your expenditure on the children – which will include a proportion of your general house outgoings – so keep a separate accounts book and note down what you spend and keep receipts for major items.

The courts will not provide any windfall benefit for the children – i.e. that they would not expect to receive if the marriage had continued. In some cases, however, where the father has persistently and wilfully failed to maintain the children, the courts can effectively 'capitalize' the children's claims by giving the custodial parent more of a share of the house sale proceeds, for example, if there is property involved.

Amounts of maintenance awarded are not usually very high – an order of £1,750 per annum for a child of, say, ten is fairly common with parents of an average joint income of £13,000 per annum.

TAX TIP

Up to mid-1988, court orders could be utilized to maximize children's tax allowances. Each child is entitled to an individual single person's tax free allowance in his or her own right. A court order for maintenance to or for a child makes that maintenance 'drop out' of the *payer's* income (off the higher rates of tax bracket where appropriate) and constitute the *child's* own income.

Nowadays, income paid to a child or to a parent on the child's behalf, is not taxable in the hands of the payee but still forms part of the payer's income. No longer does any adjustment need to be made for maintenance payments 'gross' or 'net' of tax – the amount specified in the court order should be paid in full without any deductions.

If you and your spouse agree maintenance you can apply at court for a *consent order* on consent applications prepared by your solicitors (with both of you also filing a statement or summary of your financial circumstances). Usually, neither of you will need to attend court.

PRE-DIVORCE

The custodial parent can apply to the local magistrates' court by 'laying a complaint' that the father has wilfully failed to pay maintenance. The court clerk will fix a hearing date which both parties and any legal representatives should attend to give evidence of each party's means. A cautionary note: because magistrates' courts tend to deal with people in lower income brackets, their orders for maintenance are often lower than those of divorce courts. Some people also dislike the atmosphere of magistrates' courts, tainted as they are with the connotation of criminality. The advantages are that the court procedure is quicker and less cumbersome and if the payer fails to pay the court bailiff will himself take steps to enforce payment (compared with divorce courts where the payee has to enforce unpaid maintenance herself).

If you agree on the amount of maintenance with your spouse,

you can apply under Section 6 of the Domestic Proceedings and Magistrates Courts Act 1978 for a Consent Order. Court attendance by the complainant (i.e. the payee) is still required.

Co-habitees

The law with regard to children has been fundamentally changed by the passing of the Family Law Reform Act 1987, which was brought in specifically to eliminate legal discrimination against children born to unmarried parents. At the time of going to press, those sections of the Act which bring in radical alternatives to the old style 'Affiliation Proceedings' had not yet been brought into force. As this is a rapidly changing area of the law, you must obtain up-to-date advice from your solicitor or other adviser to see what applications would be open to you.

AFFILIATION PROCEEDINGS

Only 'single women', i.e. women who are single or were single at the time of the birth of the child, can apply for maintenance for their 'illegitimate' (a concept which is due to be abolished insofar as is possible by the 1987 Act) children. Applications have to be made to the local magistrates' court.

There are three stages to the application:

1. Paternity. The 'Complainant' (usually the mother, but the local authority, Secretary of State or custodian can apply) has to prove that the father (who is called the 'putative' father until his fatherhood is established) *is* the father. Evidence can include the father's name appearing on the birth certificate, an admission of paternity, or forensic proof by way of bloodtests or DNA fingerprinting (a comparatively new and very accurate type of test – see page 172 under 'Cellmark Diagnostics' for the UK address of the company which offers this service. You will need to check the current price.).

2. Determination of amount of maintenance. The mother

will usually give evidence to the court about her own financial circumstances and as much about the father's circumstances as she is aware. The father can attend court to tell the magistrates about his own position, providing documentary evidence wherever possible. The court can, however, determine the amount in the father's absence.

3. Consideration of how maintenance should be paid. Usually, maintenance payments are ordered to be paid weekly.

Limitations

Affiliation proceedings have to be brought within three years of the birth of the child or within three years of the date that voluntary maintenance payments were last made. Any lump sum claimed, as opposed to maintenance, is limited to £500.

THE NEW LAW

Under the Family Law Reform Act 1987, either the father or the mother can apply for maintenance for a child, whether its parents were or were not married. Applications will be able to be made to the magistrates', county or high courts, whichever provides the most suitable forum. There will be a much wider choice of remedies too. Not only can applications be made for maintenance, which can be secured, but also for lump sums (with no initial limit) and property adjustment orders.

Taking the Children Abroad

Whether you are off to Spain for a week or thinking of emigrating, the following rules apply:

For ex-married parents	For co-habitees
If the divorce is underway and Section 41 certificate granted, you must obtain the written consent of your ex-partner or a	If you are going on holiday, there is usually no problem, but a wise move is to obtain the other parent's written consent in

court order to be able to take your children abroad (or even to Scotland). While this rule is often ignored, the law says you must get consent or an order every time your child goes outside England and Wales. If your ex-partner is unreasonably withholding consent, apply to the court on notice with a supporting affidavit setting out your reasons.

advance. If you take your children abroad without the other parent's consent, that parent can ask the court to review your decision, for example in wardship proceedings.

Never consider abducting your child abroad without the agreement of the other parent. By so doing, you will be deliberately cutting off your child's roots and may well also be guilty of a criminal offence under the Child Abduction Act 1984.

Danger: Wardship

Any interested party can make a child (under eighteen) a ward of court. From the moment that the necessary legal documents are filed, the court becomes the legal 'parent' of the child. If you then take a ward of court outside England and Wales without the court's consent, you are in 'contempt of court' (a potentially imprisonable offence). If you or your ex-partner do not want the child to go abroad, wardship proceedings are a way of putting a spanner in the works (also see page 103 on child abduction and kidnapping).

Changing a Child's Surname

It is important from the child's viewpoint that he or she maintains links with his or her natural father. A surname is one of the strongest links between child and father and gives the child a sense of his or her own identity, a sense of belonging. Consider a change of surname very carefully and go ahead only if the paternal relationship is very tenuous *and* the child has become a completely integral part of a new family. If the real reason is to overcome your embarrassment and it is not really in your child's best interests, forget the thought of changing the surname.

For ex-married parents: in usual circumstances, the mother has to apply to the court – a divorce court if divorce proceedings have been commenced, otherwise the local county court. The court is unlikely to grant an application for a change of name unless you have very persuasive grounds for so doing. Normally the court will insist on the consent of the natural father and you need to get confirmation of such consent by an agreement in writing signed and dated by the father. Even if the natural father has disappeared, you should apply to the court.

For ex-cohabitees: a mother can normally change her child's surname without the consent of the natural father. It is best to execute a change of name deed poll which confirms the change (this will cost about £40 from your local solicitor).

Steps to Take

A name is established first of all by custom and usage. Start calling your child by the new surname and make sure everyone else does. Change all records – medical, school and passport if necessary. The passport office will want a copy of the deed poll, agreement from the father or court order. It is not possible to change the birth certificate.

Independent Voluntary Conciliation

As an alternative method of problem-solving, you could well consider, with your partner, approaching a local conciliation agency (many of which are affiliated to the NFCC, see page 175. The purpose of a conciliator or mediator is to assist separating parents to come to their own mutually acceptable solution to the family's difficulties. The process is voluntary and confidential; it cannot subsequently be referred to in any litigation.

PART FOUR

LEGALITIES

Having worked out what you wish or have to do practically and emotionally, your intentions may now need to be 'translated' into legal processes. For co-habitees, the path is comparatively straightforward – there is no legal hoop through which you have to jump to end the relationship, although you may still need to apply to the court concerning the children (see page 79) or property (see pages 127 ff.) if you cannot resolve those issues amicably with your ex-partner. For spouses, to put an end to the marriage you have to institute divorce proceedings. Once begun, within the context of divorce proceedings, you can deal with any disagreements concerning finance or the children by way of applications to the divorce court. The various financial actions open to you are dealt with in Chapter 11.

There are other circumstances where you may be forced to seek relief from the court in an emergency – namely, domestic violence and child kidnapping. Applications to stop your partner from harassing you (non-molestation injunctions) or to exclude him from the home (ouster orders) are covered on pages 98 ff. Child abduction is dealt with on pages 103 ff.

9   Divorce Proceedings

You cannot bring divorce proceedings until one year has elapsed since the date of the marriage. Under present legislation, one of you (husband or wife) has to petition the court for a divorce. This partner is then called the *petitioner*. The other partner becomes the *respondent*. A *co-respondent* is a person named in the petition as having had an adulterous relationship with the respondent. You cannot yet make a joint divorce application to the court although this has been recommended by the Law Commission.

Grounds for a Divorce

First the good news: there is only one ground on which you can start off divorce proceedings namely the 'irretrievable breakdown' of the marriage. Now the bad: you have to *prove* irretrievable breakdown by alleging one of five 'facts', which are: (1) adultery; (2) unreasonable behaviour; (3) desertion for two years; (4) separation for two years with consent; (5) separation for five years.

The marriage must really be over before you can bring divorce proceedings. If you are still living with your spouse under the same roof, you must show that you are leading separate lives, i.e. not making love or sharing the same bed, not eating together or doing the shopping for each other, not doing each other's washing or other household chores. If you have no choice but to carry on living at the same address for a while, arrangements to separate can seem artificial at first. For example, one of you will have to move into another room to sleep and you should cook using separate pans in the kitchen. You must, however, delineate boundaries to stop you being a couple.

Of the five facts, only the first two are available to spouses who have not spent a period of two years apart.

1.   Adultery

There are two parts to this – first that the respondent has committed adultery and secondly that you find it intolerable to live with him or her. You must have known of the adultery for less than six months. Otherwise, if you have lived with your husband/wife for more than six months after you became aware of the relationship, you will be taken to have accepted the adultery and you will not be able to start off divorce proceedings under this fact.

If you know whom your spouse has been sleeping with, you must name that person as a co-respondent and copies of the divorce petition will be served on him or her. If you do not know, the divorce petition should include all known facts you are aware of (for example saying a forename and where you understand the relationship to have taken place). You could refer to the co-respondent in the petition by phrases such as 'a co-respondent whose name and identity are known only as Fiona' or 'a co-respondent whose name and full identity are unknown to the petitioner'.

2.   Unreasonable Behaviour

This is the short form by which the second fact is generally known. The full fact is as follows: 'that the respondent has behaved in such a way that the petitioner cannot reasonably be expected to live with him or her.'

Unreasonable behaviour can cover a wide variety of sins and omissions, for example violence, alcoholism, workaholism, re-fusal to spend time together, excessive demands for or refusal of sex. Petitions on this 'fact' are usually drafted to state the patterns of unreasonable behaviour in general terms and then to cite some specific instances, for example:

The Respondent frequently drinks to excess, having no regard for the distress thereby occasioned to the Petitioner. On or around January 1st 1984 the Respondent drank a bottle and a half of whisky and thereafter vomited in the hallway of the former matrimonial home and insulted the Petitioner, referring to her, inter alia, as 'an old slag', causing the Petitioner great distress and embarrassment.

Make a point of including recent instances of unreasonable behaviour; if you and your spouse have been living together for more than six months after the last incident alleged, the court may ask for further evidence before granting a divorce.

The courts these days tend to take a pragmatic view. If you are living apart and it is clear that the marriage is over, the standard that you have to comply with to fall within the heading of unreasonable behaviour is not particularly high. Where however your spouse has behaved like an angel (which can be infuriating in its own way) you may have to wait until you have lived apart for at least two years before applying for a divorce, if your spouse will not apply for a divorce against you.

All of the following three grounds involve a period of at least two years' separation.

3.   Desertion for Two Years

Rarely used, under this ground your partner must have left you, against your will, for a period of at least two years.

4.   Separation for Two Years with Consent

Often referred to as the 'no fault' ground, you and your spouse must have lived separate and apart for a period of at least two years and your spouse must consent to the divorce going through.

5.   Separation for Five Years

If you do not 'qualify' under any of the grounds outlined above, you have to wait until you and your spouse have lived apart for a period of five years. But, husbands beware. Wives can hold up the finalization of the divorce under this ground by lodging a Section 10 notice asking the court not to grant a divorce on the grounds of 'grave financial or other hardship'. You are likely to get your divorce in the end, but in the meantime this puts a spanner in the works.

Living Together

If, after you and your spouse have lived apart, you attempt a reconciliation which then subsequently does not work, you will have to calculate carefully whether the periods of time you have lived apart qualify. If you live together for more than six months, time stops running to qualify under the latter three heads and you will have to wait for another full period of at least two years to expire before filing a divorce petition. For periods of reconciliation amounting to less than six months, add the total time together to a period of two years before you start off proceedings. (For example if you have lived together for one month after having ten months apart, then you split up again for a second time, you will have to wait for another fourteen months before filing your divorce under fact 4. It will be two years and one month from the date you first separated before you can apply for a divorce.)

Which Ground is Best?

If you have any choice in the matter, unreasonable behaviour petitions and to a lesser extent adultery petitions tend to start off the divorce on a sour note. The two-year separation divorce casts no fault on either side and so often proceeds more amicably, although sometimes there are valid reasons why you cannot wait that long. Five-year separation petitions tend to be used as a last resort if you do not qualify under any of the other grounds.

The Process of Divorce Proceedings

The process of a no problem (uncontested) divorce is described in a flowchart overleaf.

WHERE DO I START?

Usually, with a solicitor who will be able to assess whether you have grounds for a divorce. A solicitor can ease the trauma of getting a divorce by writing to your partner in advance in an endeavour to obtain preliminary agreement on at least some of the issues. The draft of a divorce petition can be agreed before it is lodged at court to minimize any potential bitterness.

WHERE DOES IT HAPPEN?

Divorce proceedings can be filed at any county court in England and Wales. Usually the documents are filed in your local divorce county court (check to see that your local court deals with divorce: some don't) or in the Divorce Registry, Somerset House, London WC2 if you live in London. If your spouse contests the divorce and it becomes 'defended', your case will be transferred automatically to the high court.

DO I NEED TO ATTEND THE COURT?

If you have no children and your partner agrees to the divorce and files an Acknowledgment of Service saying so, then you do not need to attend court to get your divorce, although you may be required to go if you have a battle over finance. The divorce proceeds by way of paperwork only under the inaptly named 'special procedure' – there is nothing special about it. If you

Flowchart for Uncontested Divorce

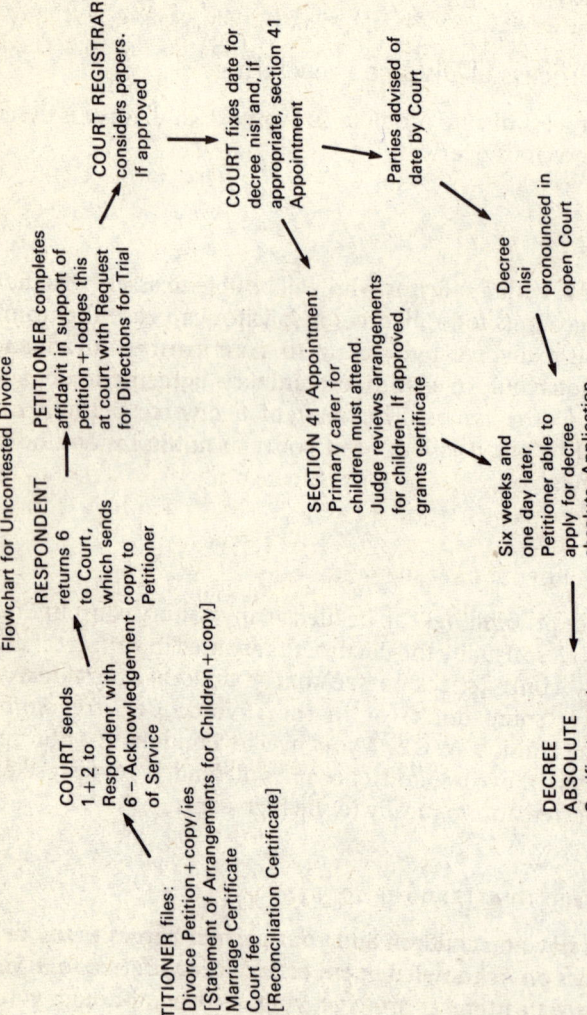

Flowchart for Uncontested Divorce

PETITIONER files:
1 – Divorce Petition + copy/ies
2 – [Statement of Arrangements for Children + copy]
3 – Marriage Certificate
4 – Court fee
5 – [Reconciliation Certificate]

COURT sends 1 + 2 to Respondent with 6 – Acknowledgement copy to Petitioner

RESPONDENT returns 6 to Court, which sends copy to Petitioner

PETITIONER completes affidavit in support of petition + lodges this at court with Request for Directions for Trial

COURT REGISTRAR considers papers. If approved

COURT fixes date for decree nisi and, if appropriate, section 41 Appointment

SECTION 41 Appointment Primary carer for children must attend. Judge reviews arrangements for children. If approved, grants certificate

Parties advised of date by Court

Decree nisi pronounced in open Court

Six weeks and one day later, Petitioner able to apply for decree absolute. Application + court fee lodged at court

DECREE ABSOLUTE Certificate sent to parties

have children, you will have to attend one appointment before the judge which is called a Section 41 Appointment (see page 71) if arrangements for them are agreed. Again, you may face attendance at court if you have to undergo legal proceedings over finance or the children.

WHAT IF MY PARTNER WON'T GIVE ME A DIVORCE?

As long as you can prove irretrievable breakdown of the marriage through facts 1, 2, 3 or 5, you should still get your divorce. If you have only recently separated and your partner hasn't had another relationship and won't agree to an unreasonable behaviour petition, you can still start off proceedings under fact 2 if you have sufficient grounds. The divorce papers will then be served upon your spouse, who should state in the Acknowledgment of Service whether he or she will defend the divorce proceedings. If your partner stubbornly sticks to his or her guns, the case will be transferred to the high court and ultimately there will be a full public hearing.

There are very few defended divorces which proceed to a full hearing – normally only about fifty in any one year, although one in fifty divorces starts out as a defended case. Most settle along the way and if, in fact, the marriage is over the courts will be pragmatic and give you a divorce if your case is presented in the right way. It is essential that your paperwork is 'pleaded' or drafted correctly – you must see a solicitor at this point. Again, it is open to you to wait for five years.

CAN I DO IT MYSELF?

The simple answer is 'yes' and the divorce court staff will be able to assist you in completing the relevant forms. You will find at the court a helpful leaflet on taking divorce proceedings yourself. Where children and/or finances are concerned you should at least take preliminary advice from a solicitor, as mistakes can be costly and time-consuming.

HOW LONG WILL IT TAKE?

Lawyers invariably take refuge behind the phrase 'it depends'.

It is very difficult at the outset to predict how long it will take from filing of proceedings to decree absolute, and for the finalization of any contested issues over finance or the children. For an undefended divorce, where there are no arguments about children or money, a typical time span will be about four to five months. With a considerable amount of extra effort this can be reduced to, say, two months. If you have to get divorced to be able to re-marry so that a child you are expecting can be born in wedlock, for example, you can apply to reduce the time between decree nisi and decree absolute, which is usually six weeks. A lot of running around at court is entailed trying to speed up the process. The average time can be added to by any one of a number of factors which can be as simple as delay by either party in dealing with the paperwork. If you foresee legal battles over custody and finance it can take several years before everything is sorted out, which highlights once again the necessity of sorting things out in advance wherever possible.

The Costs and Paying for Them

A do-it-yourself divorce for non-legally-aided parties costs about £55. (Court filing fee: £40.00; plus affidavit swearing fee: £3.75; plus court application fee for decree absolute: £10.00.) Contact the court to check on the exact fees.

For those qualifying for legal aid without any contribution under the Green Form of legal aid (see page 95), it costs nothing.

For those instructing solicitors: a simple divorce in London can range from about £250 to £600. Outside London the costs may well be less. For battle-hungry clients or partners unlucky enough once to have been married to them, the cost can run into the thousands. Again you may be able to qualify for legal aid which will at least reduce your outlay (see page 96).

Lawyers do not come cheap. Even if you qualify for legal aid, the Law Society, which administers the legal aid fund, will in most circumstances claw back your legal costs from any property allocated to you over the value of £2,500, under what is known as the 'statutory charge'. Legal aid alleviates only the necessity of paying legal costs up front. None the less, to obtain the services of a lawyer who knows what he or she is doing and who acts in your best interests is a worthwhile investment for the future.

Paying Privately

Your legal fees will usually be assessed on an hourly basis, i.e. how much of your lawyer's *time* has been involved. Be careful to use your solicitor's time wisely. It is better to avoid an expensive, rambling telephone conversation by sending your solicitor a precise and more economical letter of instruction. Hourly rates vary enormously, from, say, £35 per hour to well over £150, to which must be added VAT and other 'disbursements' or out-of-pocket expenses, like the fixed fees payable on the issue of court applications. Your solicitor may advise you that it is necessary to take a barrister's advice, in which case the barrister's fees will be added to your bill. Be sure to ask your solicitor what hourly rates he or she charges and whether there will be any extra cost for letters sent to or from the solicitor and whether there will be any percentage 'mark up' or uplift at the end of the case to reflect its complexity. You can ask to be billed on an interim basis of, say, every two months to ensure that the final bill is not unmanageable.

In some circumstances your solicitor may be prepared to wait until there is a final division of the assets before rendering a bill but if you do intend to follow this path, make sure you are not lulled into a false sense of security. The final bill is likely to be high. Clarify at the outset how payment of costs will be managed – it will save you and your solicitor heartaches later.

WHAT IF I OBJECT TO THE BILL?

Speak to your solicitor about it directly at first. He or she may be willing to reduce the bill if, and only if, you have valid arguments against it (not just because you do not like the look of it). If you do not reach agreement, you can write to ask your solicitor to obtain a 'remuneration certificate' from the Law Society if your case is non-contentious, namely, not involved around litigation. More likely, if your case was contentious, you have the right to apply to the court within one month after the invoice date of the bill to get the bill 'taxed'. A court registrar (or Taxing Master) will then look at the bill and decide if you have been overcharged.

WILL I HAVE TO PAY MY PARTNER'S LEGAL COSTS?

In many cases, particularly if you are the respondent in divorce proceedings based on adultery or unreasonable behaviour, an order that you should pay the petitioner's costs 'to be taxed if not agreed' will be made. If you have fought a contested battle over finance, and lost, again you may have to pay the other side's costs, taxed if not agreed. Costs, in legal jargon, tend to 'follow the event' – in effect the winner takes all – unless you are involved in litigation over custody or access, where orders for costs are rarely made. If an order for costs is made against you, you have the right to ask for the other solicitor's detailed account and then apply for it to be taxed if you disagree with the amount. The sum of 'taxed costs' usually amounts to around 60–80 per cent of the actual bill rendered to a client – so even if you 'win', you are likely to have to pick up the tab, if you are paying privately, for the balance of your own solicitor's bill.

Legal Aid

There are three types of legal aid in matrimonial cases where, if your application is approved, the legal aid fund will meet or promise to meet your solicitor's costs in advance. However, if you recover or preserve property worth more than £2,500 as a result of the proceedings where you were legally aided, your legal costs will be deducted from capital received by you or added as a charge to your home where it is not sold. This is known as the Law Society's 'statutory charge'.

These days, there are fewer solicitors willing to take on legal aid cases as they get paid less than private cases and there are added administrative burdens. Check in advance if your solicitor acts for legally-aided clients. There can be disadvantages in being a legally-aided client, mostly because of the delays occasioned by waiting until your application is processed (between four weeks and several months) and thereafter by having to obtain the Law Society's authority to take any out-of-the-ordinary steps in the proceedings.

However, there is one great plus factor. If you are able to get legal aid and your partner cannot qualify, you have a tactical advantage if your partner is restricted in the payment of private legal aid costs. You appear in a stronger position and the very fact of your being legally aided is an incentive for your partner to settle, perhaps on more advantageous terms for you.

There are several types of legal aid.

1. THE GREEN FORM

So called because of the colour of the form you sign (not everything involved with lawyers is complicated!), this covers you for initial advice and assistance, which can include your solicitor advising on a first interview, preparing divorce papers and writing a few letters. It will not cover you for litigation which is an area covered by a full-blown legal-aid certificate, but your solicitor can assist you in completing the legal aid application forms within the scope of the green form.

The financial limits for the provision of green form advice are tight. Your solicitor will assess on the spot whether you qualify under both the capital and income limits. He or she will assess your *disposable income* and your *capital*. You have to be under limits on both counts, although if you are in receipt of supplementary benefit or family income supplement you only have to pass the test on capital.

'Disposable income' is your *weekly income* less deductions for *tax* and *National Insurance* and for *fixed amounts*. (If you are supporting your spouse and have dependent children the fixed amounts deducted for each child depends on his or her age.)

If your disposable income is below certain limits, your green form advice will be free. Above that limit you will have to pay a contribution (payable immediately to your solicitor) assessed on a sliding scale.

The capital which will be taken into account is all of your capital resources excluding your home and its contents, the tools of your trade, personal effects and the subject matter over which you require advice (for example, if your partner has made a claim against a capital sum, that sum can be ignored).

There are limits on the maximum 'disposable' allowable capital which increase if you have dependents.

2.   ASSISTANCE BY WAY OF REPRESENTATION (ABWOR)

If your case is to be heard in the magistrates' courts, in addition to the green form, you will need to fill in one other form. A legal aid officer will assess whether or not you should be granted a certificate. Income limits are the same as for the green form, but the capital limits are slightly relaxed, again with greater limits available to you if you have dependents.

The rates vary from year to year so check with your solicitor or local Advice Centre for further information.

3.   FULL LEGAL AID

A full legal aid certificate can only be applied for annexed to court proceedings, but if you qualify it will cover all your legal costs in the first instance (solicitor's fees, barrister's fees if necessary and even accountancy fees if you need an accountant to investigate the marital financial position). Legal aid is *not* granted for undefended divorce cases per se.

Through your solicitor, you apply to the local legal aid area office by completing two forms. One is the application itself and the other summarizes your means. If this is an emergency situation, you will also need to complete a third form, an emergency application. Your means will be assessed by the DHSS who may well call you for an interview if your financial position is complicated. If your position is straightforward, your application will be dealt with on paperwork only. Again, you may have to make a contribution, but, if so, this will be spread out over a period of twelve monthly instalments. Whether or not your case merits the issuing of a full certificate will be decided by officers of the local legal aid area office.

The calculation for income limits is similar to that necessary for the green form, although the ceiling is slightly higher. Your own, not your spouse's, annual income will be assessed and then deductions will be made in respect of the following: income tax and National Insurance contributions; job expenses including travel costs and union subscriptions; rent or mortgage repayments and rates; HP repayments; and insurance premiums.

The capital limits are also much higher. Check with your solicitor or local Advice Centre for current figures.

Note: If your financial position changes (this can include re-marriage), your entitlement to legal aid may well be affected – check with your solicitor.

IN SUMMARY

Even if you do qualify for legal aid, you need to take care that your legal costs do not go through the roof. The warnings contained in the 'paying privately' section apply equally here. Fight in the courts only if you have to; reasonable negotiation can work wonders and always saves money.

Watch out for changes in Legal Aid: The Legal Aid Act has changed the law slightly, particularly with reference to the statutory charge. Check with your solicitor for details.

10 Emergency Relief

Domestic Violence

This section applies both to people who have been married or co-habiting. The legal routes you might take to achieve the same end may differ, but the results and the practical angles are usually precisely the same.

Violence is born from extreme frustration and a tendency to be unable to communicate or get what is wanted by any other means. Violent men are frustrated, angry people who are driven to assert their 'dominance' over their partners in the only way they feel is left to them, through their greater physical strength. A tiny minority of women resort to violence, again out of frustration, often taking advantage of their partner having vowed never to hit a woman. For the sake of simplicity and to reflect the majority, violent partners are referred to as he, their victims as she.

Society has been ambivalent in the past about violence in domestic relationships, paying lip-service to its public condemnation while failing to provide victims with the support they required from the police and other services. Domestic violence cuts across all strata of society. It tends to occur more frequently where patterns of violence have already been established, whether in the relationship itself or in the childhood of either partner. Very often violence is linked to abuse of some kind, usually alcohol. The chaos and emotional tension of separation can themselves be sufficient to trigger off a violent outburst. However violence arises, you need to take steps to protect yourself.

Advice to Victims

Domestic violence almost always flares up behind closed doors, with no one else to see what has happened. You must get out of a situation where you are suffering violence as quickly as possible.

LEAVING THE HOME

In a case of dire emergency, you should leave the home. Remember, it is always possible to get a court order to say your partner should leave the house, so that you are not forced to go, but if you need to protect yourself immediately, leave the home. Contact your local homeless families service (listed as 'Housing' under your local authority in the telephone directory, e.g. London Borough of Camden – Housing) or the social services department of your local authority or contact Women's Aid (see telephone number on page 176). Women's refuges are for all female victims of violence. They provide a roof to sleep under and a bed or even a floor to sleep on only. As both local authorities and women's refuges tend to be tight on financial resources, see if you can spend the night with a relative or friend who will provide a safe haven. Make sure your partner does not know where you are.

LEAVING THE CHILDREN

Take them with you if at all possible. If you have not made yourself intentionally homeless, the local authority is duty bound to re-house you and women's refuges will always find a space for children. Where you have no option but to leave them, do not panic. However, take immediate action by contacting a solicitor to get the children back.

CHANGING THE LOCKS

If you jointly own or rent the home with your partner, you have no instant 'right' to lock him out. If you do change the locks he may be able to get a court order restoring him to the home. He cannot, however, legally break into the home by violent means. If your partner has been violent you can apply to the court to force him out of the house. Once he has left, change the locks.

CONTACTING THE POLICE

The police gained a poor reputation in the past by being unwilling to assist victims of what they perceived to be domestic problems. Now their attitude is changing. In London, the Metropolitan Police have to record every violent incident in a special book and investigate it (this can provide useful corroborative evidence later in court). Elsewhere, there are some signs of change. The police can not only intervene in the fight but may also assist later once court proceedings have been taken; for example, in escorting you back to the house and ensuring that an injunction is complied with if you have a power of arrest attached to it. So, dial 999.

MEDICAL REPORTS AND OTHER WITNESSES

If you are injured, even just bruised, go and see your doctor or the casualty department of your local hospital and make sure you are physically examined and your injuries noted on medical records. Medical records provide useful evidence in any court proceedings and even if you decide later not to go to court, the evidence will be there for you to rely on in the future, if need be.

If anyone other than you and your partner has witnessed the violence, ask if he or she would be willing to come forward as a witness.

CONTACTING A SOLICITOR

It is essential that you see a solicitor as soon as possible after the incident, to get advice. If you wait a few weeks, your remedies are likely to be severely curtailed. If, after telling the solicitor what happened, he or she thinks you have a strong enough case to go to court and you decide to do so, the solicitor will prepare an affidavit (a sworn statement) or affidavits for you and for any witnesses and then will make the appropriate application. You can apply for either or both of: (1) *a non-molestation injunction* which stops your partner from interfering with or harassing you. This can include him being ordered not to communicate with you save through solicitors; (2) *an ouster order* which orders your partner out of the house or confines him to a specified limited area. This can be extended so your partner cannot approach a given area around the home, for example a radius of 100 yards.

THE PROCEDURE

The law provides a rather confusing variety of remedies. Married persons' applications for non-molestation injunctions can be made within divorce proceedings in the divorce court, in the magistrates' court under the Domestic Proceedings and Magistrates Court Act 1978, or in the county court under the Domestic Violence and Matrimonial Proceedings Act 1976. Co-habitees can also use the latter remedy if they were 'living together' when the application was made to the court (which can cover you for ouster orders too). If, as an ex-cohabitee, you have not been living together with your partner recently, you may be able to get an injunction annexed to a claim for trespass or another tort. Applications for ouster orders are usually made for a wife under the Matrimonial Homes Act 1983 in the county court or under the Domestic Proceedings and Magistrates Court Act 1978 in the magistrates' court. Your solicitor will advise which remedy is most appropriate for you.

'EX-PARTE' OR 'ON NOTICE'

If the violence or threat of it has been severe, you can go to court with your legal representatives and ask for a non-molestation order *without telling your partner*. In extreme circumstances, you can even ask the court that he or she should be put out of the home. This is known as an 'ex-parte' application. If you get your injunction, this will have to be served together with the other court proceedings on your partner and the court will fix a return date, normally in a week's time, for your partner to be given the opportunity to put his side of the case. This latter hearing is thus 'on notice'. If the violence has not been extreme, the usual first application is 'on notice'. Courts do seem to be tightening up and are less willing to grant an 'ex-parte' injunction.

You are likely to be called to the witness box if the judge or magistrate wishes to question you further about your affidavit or if your partner defends the allegations you have made against him. The judge or magistrate will then decide whether you have proved your case for an injunction or if the matter could be dealt with by, for example, the giving of undertakings (see below).

Injunctions used to be limited in time for, say, three to six months. Nowadays the courts seem to be more willing in certain circumstances to make the injunction last for an indefinite period. The injunction will lapse automatically if you and your partner get back together again.

A POWER OF ARREST

Where you have suffered an assault from your partner and there is a real danger of your being assaulted again, the court will grant a power of arrest, which enables the police to arrest your partner immediately if he breaches the injunction. Powers of arrest normally last for fixed periods of three to six months.

What Happens if You Have been Served with an Injunction

If you have been violent towards your partner in the past or know that the level of tension is rising to such a level that you feel yourself wanting to lash out, you are at risk of being violent in the future. Whenever a flashpoint occurs or is likely to occur, get yourself out of the situation immediately. Be responsible for your actions. Leave the home if necessary for a cooling-off period. If you are addicted in some way or another, for example an alcoholic, take steps to overcome that addiction. It is no use drinking yourself into oblivion, behaving violently and then later pleading you cannot remember what happened. The courts will be more predisposed to order you out of the house if you are placing your partner at risk of physical or mental abuse.

LEGALLY

If you are served with an injunction, read it carefully, together with any other documents given to you, for example the application and the affidavit. See a solicitor as soon as possible and make an appointment as much in advance of the hearing date as you can. Some solicitors will not act for violent men and you will have to check this in advance. The solicitor will take a statement from you and transform this into an affidavit. If the allegations made against you are seriously wrong, you can defend your case in court and ask the judge or magistrate not to make an order against you. You will have to prepare your case very thoroughly. You can offer to give an *undertaking* to the court not to molest your partner, and avoid having an order made against you. Breaking the terms of an undertaking can invoke just as serious a penalty as breaking the terms of a court order.

Child Abduction

Since the passing of the 1984 Child Abduction Act, you may be committing a criminal offence by taking a child out of the country without the written consent of the other parent. For ex-cohabitees, this Act does not normally apply unless the child has been abducted from the mother (who is usually viewed by the courts as having custody of the child) or there is a custody order in favour of the father.

Your remedies, however, are not limited to the Child Abduction Act. If, for any valid reason, you feel there is a real and imminent danger of your child being taken out of the country by the other parent, you can telephone the police or go to your local police station and insist upon the police carrying out a procedure known as a 'port alert'. Under this, the police are obliged to notify all airports and seaports of the danger of your child being taken out of the country. You should take with you to the police station a photograph of the child or a full description, full details of his or her name and address and date of birth and a description of the potential abductor.

This remedy can be useful but has been found to be ineffective where a child has been taken out of a port where there is major traffic, for example one of the cross-Channel ports where it is difficult for customs officials to intercept potential abductors.

Wardship Proceedings

If you feel your child is likely to be abducted, every minute counts and you must see a solicitor as soon as possible. Once the child has been taken out of the country, it is far more difficult to ensure he or she is returned.

Telephone your solicitor and get him or her to make the child a ward of court (see page 81). Immediately upon issuing of the wardship proceedings, your child will become a ward and the court in effect becomes the legal parent of that child. You will also need, however, to get a court order stating that the child should not be removed from the jurisdiction (i.e. England and Wales) without the court's consent. If you know when the child is being taken out of the country by any chance (for example, if you have heard the father is planning to take him out of Heathrow on a flight at ten o'clock to the United States) you can then get your solicitor to ensure that an order is served upon the father if there is sufficient time. As long as you manage to get hold of a solicitor, the courts are even prepared to 'sit' outside usual court opening times (10 A.M. to 4 P.M.); your solicitor may be able to trace a judge (a duty judge) and telephone him or her at home and get an order made.

11 Financial Proceedings

This chapter covers what happens if:

1. You have started divorce proceedings and either (a) you have agreed everything with your partner (see 'For Spouses Who Agree: Consent Orders', page 106) or (b) nothing or not everything is agreed and a fight may be in prospect (see 'For Spouses Who Cannot Agree', page 107).
2. You are not married and you have to resort to forcing your ex-partner to divide the property equitably (see pages 127 ff.).

The Approach

Before you leap into the boxing ring of litigation, you need to prepare your ground carefully. You should consult a solicitor now if you have not already done so. The solicitor can put forward proposals to your partner or his or her solicitors and negotiate towards an agreement.

Only a very few claims in divorce proceedings (less than 10 per cent) actually get into court for a final hearing. Settlements are often made along the way, even on the steps outside court. At that late stage, the savings in legal costs are minimal; earlier, you can achieve considerable reductions. A solicitor who adopts a conciliatory approach (as recommended by the Solicitors' Family Law Association) can be a powerful ally.

First you must consider whether you need to protect your position. If the house is in the sole name of the husband, the wife can now register a caution against dealings against the title of the property, if it is registered, at HM Land Registry, or a Class F Land Charge if the property is unregistered (see page 7). This will prevent the husband from selling the property without the wife's prior knowledge or from borrowing further against the security of the home.

If the husband is threatening to dispose of assets, the wife can also get an injunction stopping him from doing so. Through a solicitor, she can apply under Section 37 of the Matrimonial Causes Act 1973 for an order from the court preventing the husband from disposing of any matrimonial assets, for example, selling a family business, giving antiques or paintings away, giving money to friends or relatives. This application is normally made *ex-parte* (see page 167) with a supporting affidavit from the wife. The court again then fixes a return date and the husband can ask for some of the assets which have been frozen to be released for him for essential purposes.

You should also consider your position, particularly if there are jointly-held accounts or you have joint credit cards: what will happen if either of you starts running up debts? You should ensure that your affairs are as separated as possible prior to starting court proceedings.

Your solicitor will be able to advise you on all of these matters.

CAUTION: A word of warning to recalcitrant spouses who intend to spirit away some of the family heirlooms (or money). The court can set aside any transaction within three years of the hearing if the transaction was carried out with the intention of depriving your partner. Also, your partner will be entitled to investigate your position (for example, by insisting upon production of the last three years' bank statements) through a process known as *discovery*. This is in addition to your obligation to file an affidavit detailing your financial position. Lying under oath amounts to perjury and there are severe penalties.

For Spouses Who Agree: Consent Orders

If you and your spouse manage to reach agreement on financial issues, the terms can be drawn up in the form of minutes of agreement and consent orders approved by both sides and their solicitors and lodged at court together with a summary of both partners' financial circumstances (a Rule 76A statement). If the court has no objection to the terms, it will make the order as requested, although sometimes personal attendance at court is necessary to answer any questions the registrar might have.

Not only do you save costs this way but the consent order, because of its greater flexibility, can include undertakings by way of a preamble to the order (for example, an undertaking by a husband 'to place sufficient funds in a bank account from which standing orders pay maintenance') which a court is unlikely to insist on. Breach of an undertaking, as already mentioned, is as serious as breach of a court order itself.

Consent orders can only be later set aside if either side has failed to make a full and frank disclosure of their financial circumstances and the concealed facts would have resulted in a different order being made.

For Spouses Who Cannot Agree

If you and your spouse cannot agree on a division of the family resources, you will be well advised to begin divorce or judicial separation proceedings to enable you to use the potent powers available to you in the divorce courts.

The applications you can make are fourfold:

1.   maintenance for yourself (and your children) during the proceedings ('pending suit') and thereafter for a definite or indefinite term ('periodical payments');
2.   a lump sum (one only) for yourself (and the children);
3.   a transfer of property to yourself (and the children);
4.   an alteration of any trust or settlement.

If you are the petitioner, you will find included in the quaintly named 'Prayer' of the petition, a claim for the above financial applications. If you have put in a defence to divorce proceedings, a similar prayer is often included in your answer and/or cross petition.

To trigger off your claims, however, you need to file a Notice of Intention to Proceed (Form 11) or Form 13 if you are a respondent in undefended proceedings. A fee is payable (currently, £15) and you will also need to lodge a prepared and sworn affidavit setting out your income, including any benefits, from all sources, your property and other assets, your debts and summarizing your and your spouse's financial positions. You can refer to the checklists on pages 16–20 as an aide memoire (now you know why you did all that work in the beginning!).

Having served your Form 11 or 13, once issued by the court, on your ex-partner, together with a copy of the affidavit, your spouse should, within fourteen days of receipt, file an affidavit in reply. This 'rule' is infrequently adhered to and you will usually have to wait until after a hearing for directions (when a court registrar sets time-limits for the filing of affidavits, discovery of documents, valuations of property and so on). Once affidavits have been filed, both sides will carry out an investigation, often done by serving questionnaires on the other side, referred to as Rule 77(4) questionnaires. These can be far-reaching, calling on your partner to produce documents and answer specific (sometimes awkward) questions. You may also need to obtain professional valuations of property and for businesses. This whole process is known as *discovery*. How long it takes depends on the complexity of the case, the tenacity of each side and the inclination of either side to delay. It will usually take at least one year from the filing of your form to get a full hearing date, although you can apply for interim maintenance (by way of a temporary court order) earlier. At the final hearing, both sides, usually through their legal representatives, present their respective cases, call witnesses (for example, accountants and valuers) and the court will decide on the merits.

A useful tactic for placing pressure on your spouse to agree sensible terms with you is to send a 'Calderbank letter' to the other side. The letter is so named after Mr and Mrs Calderbank, whose lawyer first used this manoeuvre. Your solicitors, having considered the merits of your case, can offer by way of letter the terms on which you would settle. The letter is marked 'Without Prejudice': a device lawyers use to protect the negotiations from being used as evidence in court later. However, if your ex-partner rejects the offer and your case has to proceed to a full hearing, you can produce the letter to the court when arguing about who should pay legal costs. If the court has made an order in similar or less generous terms than you originally offered, it will normally order that the person who rejected that offer should bear all the costs incurred thereafter.

WHAT APPROACH DO THE COURTS ADOPT?

Litigation is inevitably a gamble. There are no 'right' answers in financial proceedings; each case depends on its own facts. This flexibility is reflected in the pragmatism of the courts' approach, summarized as that of 'needs and resources' (how long is a piece of string?).

There are certain considerations contained in Section 25 of the Matrimonial Causes Act 1973 which the court should take into account in the balancing exercise it has to carry out. Amendments to this legislation were made by the Matrimonial and Family Proceedings Act 1984 which gave two important extra guidelines: (1) that the children's needs take priority; (2) that the spouses should aim to become financially independent of each other.

The second guideline was hailed as the end of the 'meal ticket for life' for ex-wives and was given almost as much publicity as another, third, consideration whereby the courts were directed to consider the conduct of the parties if it would be 'inequitable' to disregard it.

In practice, the conduct directive has had little impact on the courts' handling of matrimonial cases. Courts are largely unconcerned with why the marriage broke down, just with what would be best to do now. However, the second consideration has influenced decisions and the minds of lawyers working in the field. Clean Break settlements are becoming increasingly popular in cases where the spouses are young, skilled and have sufficient resources to survive independently in the future.

The Clean Break

By law, a husband is under a duty to maintain his wife. In some rare cases, the reverse also works: for example, during the miners' strike, a Barnsley wife was ordered to pay £12 per week maintenance to her striking miner husband. Maintenance obligations usually continue until the point when either a court dismisses, by way of order, the potential claims for maintenance of each party or until your ex-wife remarries. If you fail to get such an order, you run the risk that in future, if your financial position improves, you could find yourself landed with a claim for income from your ex. How can this be avoided?

Through a clean break order, the wife (or in Joan Collins-style cases the husband) is allocated a larger share of the capital than she would have otherwise received to buy out her entitlement to maintenance.

If you envisage that you and your partner are able to create new lives for yourselves and you both have the capacity to do so, a clean break settlement has much to recommend it. Remember, though, that you can never stop parents' liability to maintain children during their minority.

Maintenance

In many other cases, wives have no alternative but to ask the court for maintenance. This can be expressed to be payable to the wife alone or to the children. In divorce proceedings, interim orders for maintenance are styled 'Maintenance pending suit'; while the term 'Periodical Payments' is used for maintenance under the final order once the marriage is ended (after decree absolute). Maintenance orders are almost always subject to revision unless you agree with your ex-partner in advance a fixed period during which a fixed amount is payable. Maintenance for the children can never be limited or excluded for the future – the court will always view such applications from the point of view of the best interests of the child.

NOTE: To avoid repeated and costly legal applications to the court to ask for variations of maintenance to keep pace with inflation, you can link the amount of maintenance to regularly produced statistics, such as the Taxes and Prices Index or the Retail Prices Index. Figures for the annual percentage increases are obtainable from the Central Statistical Office (see page 172).

HOW MUCH?

Again, there are no hard and fast rules, just general guidelines. The basic approach is that of 'needs and resources'. First you have to calculate the income available to be distributed and the demands that will be made on that income. Remember that both of you are likely to have to drop your standard of living. Your projections of outgoings should be based on your changed circumstances – if you are going to move to a smaller house, for example, your calculations should take into account any reductions on the bills.

If you have children, look at what their outgoings will be too. It is better to tackle the subject of maintenance globally. Whoever has care and control of the children should be able to get an order against the other parent for maintenance if he/she is able to pay.

The 'one-third guideline'

A 1973 case called *Wachtel v. Wachtel* confirmed in the Court of Appeal the principle or guideline that an ex-wife might expect to receive about a third of the parties' joint income for herself. Many cases have since disapproved of a rigid one-third rule but it remains a useful rule of thumb, where the marriage has been long-lasting.

The Courts, however, will never order a husband to pay over more than half of his income to his wife and children, however many. (More doubt has, however, been cast on this principle since the Finance Act 1988; see pages 112 ff.)

Thus, if Amy and Ben Jones earn annually £5,000 and £17,000 respectively, Amy might expect to receive top-up maintenance of £2,000 per annum (£5,000 plus £17,000 = £21,000; divided by 3 = £7,000; less £5,000 = £2,000).

'On Your Bike'

In some cases now, a wife who refuses to work but is able and qualified to obtain a job may have assigned to her a 'working capacity'. The court may presume she is able to earn the level of salary her skills would equip her for and reduce her maintenance accordingly. However, the husband will have to show that appropriate vacancies are available.

GUIDELINES FOR THE CHILDREN

There are no statutory guidelines, but lawyers are having increasing recourse to figures published by the National Foster Care Association which give an indication of the cost of bringing up a child in foster care from birth to eighteen years, both in London and the provinces.

The weekly figures for April 1988 are as follows:

Age of child (yrs)	Recommended weekly allowance in provinces (£)	Recommended weekly allowance in London (£)
0–4	30.52	33.88
5–7	35.63	39.55
8–10	39.06	43.33
11–12	42.42	47.11
13–15	45.85	50.89
16–18	61.11	67.83

TAX IMPLICATIONS

Up to the radically reforming budget of 15 March 1988 a husband could get tax relief on payments made to his wife or the children. For children's payments, he *had* to get a court order for maintenance, whether from a divorce court or from a magistrates' court. For payments made to a wife, as long as these were paid under a court order or under a deed of separation, the payments were tax deductable from the husband's viewpoint. Voluntary payments, then as now, did not attract any tax relief at all.

For orders which were *applied for* before 15 March 1988 and actually made prior to 30 June 1988, the maintenance payments were set off against the *payer's* liability to basic rate tax or higher rates of tax. The payments became taxable in the *payee's* hands only if the income allocated to each person exceeded his or her personal tax-free allowance. The children, be they ever so small, were each entitled to a single person's tax-free allowance. After separation, a husband was no longer entitled to a married man's personal tax-free allowance, but was allocated similarly a single person's allowance. A wife had the equivalent of a single person's tax-free allowance also. Whoever had care and control of the children would receive an additional allowance which represented the difference between the single person's and the married man's allowances.

With the 1988 budget, came a completely new system for taxing married couples, which also abolished the tax advantages (in the sense of being able to maximize available income) which existed under the old system. From April 1990, the Finance Act 1988 ensured that husbands and wives will be independently taxed and each will be responsible for his or her own separate income.

For court orders made after the rules of the Finance Act 1988 came into effect, the only tax relief that the payer will receive is the difference between the single person's tax-free allowance and the married man's allowance. Maintenance payments made under court orders or separation agreements remain, from the Inland Revenue's viewpoint, the income of the payer and are, subject to the above exception, taxed in his hands in the same way as he would have been taxed while still married and living with his spouse. Maintenance payments are not taxable in the hands of the payee.

At the time of writing, the Finance Act 1988 has just been introduced and so its effects can only be anticipated. It appears to be likely that maintenance payments to ex-wives and children are likely to be much reduced, bearing in mind the fact that it is no longer possible to utilize the children's and the wife's single person's tax-free allowances. For ex-wives, the one-third principle established by the case of Wachtel, is likely to be considerably eroded. Far more emphasis is likely to be placed on the husband's available income and ex-wives and children are likely to have to cope on less.

Payments under existing arrangements, including payments to children, will continue to be treated by the Inland Revenue under the present rules for the tax year 1988–9; except that people who are separated or divorced and receiving payments under existing maintenance arrangements, will be exempt from tax on the first £1,490. From 1989–90 there will be a limit to the payer's relief, based on the relief given in 1988–9, although payers will be able to choose to switch to the new system if they prefer. It is highly unlikely it will be advantageous to switch to the new system if existing court orders are already in force.

If you do have an existing court order, the tax relief that the payer is able to get in the tax year 1989–90 will effectively be frozen for the future. Thus, if you have to apply to vary maintenance payments, the payer will not get tax relief on the additional amounts ordered to be paid.

Tax is deducted at source only if payments have been made under an order existing before the 1988 budget. If so, payments should have been made less tax (i.e. deducting a notional amount for basic rate tax). Thus, using the above example for tax year 1987–8, Ben Jones, having been ordered to pay £2,000 per annum to his wife, would actually pay: £2,000 less (£2,000 × 27%) = £1,460.00 net.

This rule applied for all orders save for those which were classified as 'small maintenance payments'.

DURATION OF MAINTENANCE

Maintenance payments to a former wife continue until the expiry of a fixed term (if agreed in advance) or during joint lives or until she re-marries. Husbands can apply to vary the order and, since the 1984 Act, the courts have power to stop maintenance payments to an ex-wife even if she does not consent to it ceasing. This power has been exercised only infrequently. If a former husband finds his ex-wife has been co-habiting with another man who has been supporting her, he can go back to court. He will have to prove that the relationship is permanent and that the new partner is financially supporting her before the court will approve his application. If he can prove these elements (no easy task) the courts can put an end to his obligation.

Payments to the children usually last until they reach the age of seventeen or complete full-time education (whichever is the later). While in some cases the father's responsibility continues during further education, it may be better to ensure your child is assessed for grant purposes on the basis of his/her mother's income alone if her income is below that of her ex-husband.

ENFORCEMENT

It is one thing obtaining a court order for maintenance, quite another getting the money in your hand if you are faced with an obstinately disobedient payer, as many ex-wives know to their cost. Ex-husbands can move, change jobs or do a disappearing act. Ultimately, they can avoid paying maintenance by emigrating to a country where the courts will not enforce British orders (although the ex-wife can still catch him if he ever returns to this country). Joe Bugner provided a public example by having to pay maintenance arrears to his former wife before he could return to the ring for his unsuccessful bout with Frank Bruno in October 1987.

What remedies are available to an ex-wife?

1. Secured Periodical Payments

If your former husband is rich enough and either has a short life expectancy or is unlikely to pay, you can attach a maintenance order to a lump sum or other property. Secured periodical payments are very seldom made. If for any reason secured payments are not made, the fund or property set aside becomes forfeit.

2. Enforcement of Private Agreements

Without the added muscle of a court order, your only remedy for non-payment is to sue the payer in the county court for the debt. Useful and free reference leaflets are published by the Lord Chancellor's Department ('Small Claims in the County Court' and 'Enforcing Money Judgement in the County Court') available from your local county court.

3. Enforcement of Court Orders

Unfortunately, there are no magic formulae for squeezing money out of a broke non-payer, but there are various remedies which can help – so don't give up without a struggle.

Registration in the magistrates' courts. To lighten the burden of collection of payments, a payee can register the county or high court order in the magistrates' court for the area in which the payer resides. Payment must then be made to the court which will pass it on to the payee, and court officials will take action if any arrears start to accrue.

The advantages of this approach is that enforcement is faster, cheaper and simpler than in the other courts and you can pass responsibility for much of the paperwork on to the court officials.

The disadvantage is that you can place yourself in a lower financial league. The work of magistrates' courts tends to be involved with people in lower income brackets and these courts have a tendency to order lower payments. Remember also that the magistrates' court has the power to reduce or, worse, remit (wipe out) any arrears.

If your ex is in regular steady employment, you can ask for the most effective remedy of all – *an Attachment of Earnings*

Order. If arrears have really built up, the magistrates can order the payer's employer to deduct the amount of maintenance from his wage or salary and send it to the court for onward transmission to the payee. The court will not reduce the payer's income below a protected income level (roughly equivalent to supplementary benefit). The tactic is ineffective for obvious reasons where the payer is either self-employed, unemployed or moves around from job to job.

Using the divorce courts. Because the court is not paid direct by the payer, the payee wife has to *prove* to the court that arrears have actually built up – which can be difficult where all your maintenance payments are in cash. Be careful to keep an accurate record of all payments actually made which you can later produce in court if necessary.

The higher courts have the same powers to order attachment of earnings. In addition you can apply for garnishee, a warrant of execution or a judgement summons.

Garnishee Orders are used against a particular bank account where *warrants of execution* are against specific property (e.g. a car). If you get a garnishee order against your ex's bank account (on the obvious proviso that there is money in the account) the bank manager has to send the money to you. Warrants of execution involve the county court bailiffs attending at your ex-husband's property and seizing goods which they then sell off to pay the amount owing.

A *Judgement Summons* presents an even tougher remedy. This is a request to the county court or to the high court for a person in arrears to be sent to jail. The wife or her lawyer must prove to the court that the husband is able to, but won't pay. The threat of going to jail is normally enough – but if your ex is really pig-headed, you may still be left with empty hands and the dubious satisfaction of knowing he is in custody.

Debts: Your Legal Position

If you have not already dealt with your creditors it is all too easy to try to forget about them, thinking they will somehow go away of their own accord. But the debit side of the accounting exercise is an aspect which you ignore at your peril. You must sit down and work out what debts you and your partner have to bring the financial picture into focus when presenting your case to the court. Consider which debts you are legally responsible for and then deal with them.

The best practical tactic to adopt, broadly speaking, is to come clean. Tell your creditors (the people you owe money to) that you have separated and how much money you owe in total. Creditors will often be prepared to accept regular but smaller repayments staggered over a longer period rather than themselves having to face court proceedings to recover the debt from you. If you have a lot of debts to pay off, sort out which ones take priority and see if you are eligible to apply for any benefits (see page 140). Having a roof over your head, warmth and food are obviously high on the list. However, it can be a false economy to cancel insurance policies if you can still stretch to them. Budget for what you can afford to keep on and then stick within the budget.

Otherwise, you might consider consolidating all the debts and taking a bank or financial loan to pay them off at once and then repay the bank loan monthly over a fixed period. However, be careful not to get involved with loan sharks: make sure the initial interest repayments are reasonable and get advice from your solicitor or local Citizens' Advice Bureau before signing on the dotted line. Most credit companies, including banks, have to be registered under the Consumer Credit Act 1974 and after you have agreed the terms of the loan, you will have a few days' grace in which you can think again and repudiate the contract if it is not right for you.

JOINT RESPONSIBILITY

If you are a joint account holder, you are jointly and severally responsible for any debts on the account even if you did not spend the money. Thus, when you separate, it is a wise move to close all joint accounts and open separate sole accounts in your respective names. If you cannot agree to do that, you can effectively freeze the accounts by writing to the bank or building societies to notify them about the separation and that withdrawals cannot be made unless on the application of both of you. Otherwise, you may find the account has been depleted and your spouse has cleared the money. Stop all credit cards too – it is better to be safe than sorry.

MORTGAGES

You need to find out in whose name the house is vested (see page 7). Most are either in the husband's name alone or in joint names. Once a caution is registered by the wife, the bank or building society must inform her too of any action it intends to take, if arrears under a mortgage build up. Once substantial arrears have arisen, the mortgagee (the bank or building society) has the right to apply to the court for foreclosure, which will ultimately result in the house being sold to pay off the mortgage, even against your will. The sting in this particular tail is that the mortgagee is under no obligation to get the best price for a property, only a reasonable market price, so you and your partner can lose out.

If there are potential problems, explain the position to the bank or building society. It may even be prepared in some cases to allow you to stop making monthly repayments in the short term, if you can't afford them, while you sort out your affairs and/or sell the property. The extra interest will be added to the mortgage and the whole debt to the mortgage will be repaid on sale.

RENT

If the home is rented from a private (as opposed to local authority) landlord, check from the rent book which name is recorded as the tenant. If it is the husband's, the wife has the right to stay in the home up to the date of decree absolute if she carries on paying the rent. She can request the court to make an order transferring the tenancy into her sole name under the Matrimonial Homes Act 1983. These rights do not apply if your unmarried partner deserts you and, unless your landlord agrees to transfer the tenancy to you, you will have to leave. You will, however, have a few months' respite before you have to go as your landlord cannot force you out. He or she will have to apply to the court for a possession order, which will be against the tenant whose name appears on the rent book.

The better course is usually not to approach the landlord unless arrears have built up. If you have no statutory right for the tenancy to be transferred into your name, keep quiet about the fact that you and your partner have separated and carry on paying the rent to your landlord. If he accepts rent from you, he may, in certain limited circumstances, be deemed to have waived his right to claim possession against you. However, where arrears have built up, you should discuss the position with your landlord and see if you can pre-empt any action he intends to take.

RATES

Check to whom the rates demands are addressed. Whoever is shown (this is usually the husband) will be responsible for payment right up to decree absolute, even if he has left the home, unless he is paying maintenance to the wife specifically including an allocation for rates. If you do not pay the rates, the council will sue and they can arrange for bailiffs to seize property to cover the arrears. To avoid this, again the partner remaining should speak to the council about any debts and either make an arrangement to pay by instalments or to get a few months' breathing space while the ex-partner is pressurized into paying maintenance sufficient to pay off the debt.

ELECTRICITY, GAS AND TELEPHONE ACCOUNTS

Another precautionary measure after separation is to telephone the utility companies and ask for the accounts to be transferred into your name. You can then budget for future bills and, if you move fast, get yourself accepted as a new customer without having to pay a lump sum deposit, which you will be almost sure to have to pay if debts build up. Meters will be read and the utility companies can chase an ex-husband for payment up to the date of separation. If, unknown to you, debts have built up and you face the threat of disconnection, if there are children in the house, tell the gas and electricity boards and your local council social services department. They may be able to help out, perhaps with an emergency payment or a loan under the Social Fund.

Capital

LUMP SUM

The court can order one spouse to pay to another a sum of capital – a lump sum. This is a once-only order, you cannot apply for more than one lump sum. Less frequently, the courts order a lump sum in favour of a child – which will then be invested for him/her on trust until he/she attains majority. Lump sum orders are made sometimes to achieve a clean break settlement (referred to on page 110), to buy out an ex-wife's claims, sometimes to compensate a partner who transfers his/her interest in his/her home to his/her partner, or in other cases where one partner deserves a share of the other's accumulated assets (for example, because of the length of the marriage and the contributions made by an ex-wife). The court has also to consider the loss of any benefit either spouse would have otherwise received if the marriage had continued (usually the loss of widow's pension from her ex's employers). If a divorced spouse stands to lose benefits, the court can again allocate him or her a share of the ex-partner's assets. Pensions and other benefits are considered on page 143.

If you invest the capital you receive, the income thereby produced will be taken into consideration by the court when assessing your maintenance entitlement.

THE MATRIMONIAL HOME

The greatest battles of all tend to be over the home. The home is usually the major or only matrimonial asset and the stakes can thus be high.

Practically, what should you do after you have separated, before the divorce is completed and before you have come to some agreement? The sensible advice is to stick it out and stay in the home until an agreement is reached. If your disagreements about the house develop into a full-blown court battle, 'possession' of the matrimonial home can be very important to each participant. Staying in the home until agreement is reached and refusing to sell the home are the husband's and wife's best tactics respectively.

It is not unusual to find yourself locked out or your partner behaving so intolerably you consider changing the locks as a last desperate measure. Owners of property (whether joint or sole) and wives have a right to remain in the matrimonial home until at least decree absolute. You should not pre-empt a court decision by changing the locks unless an extreme situation arises – for example, if your children are in danger. If you are locked out, you can get an order restoring you to the home but you must act quickly and you should also consider whether that would be the best move.

The Court's Approach

There are broadly three methods of dealing with a home which is privately owned. The court can order: (1) a sale and then a division of the proceeds between husband and wife, or all the proceeds to go to one or other; (2) a transfer of the home into one partner's sole name either outright or on payment of a lump sum or subject to a deferred charge; (3) a postponed sale (e.g. until the children finish school) and then a proportionate division between husband and wife assessed usually on a percentage basis.

For properties abroad, the court will make an order only if

you can prove that it is likely to be obeyed in the country where the property is based.

There are no set rules; again, the court takes the pragmatic approach of needs and resources. The purpose is to achieve the often impossible – the creation of two homes out of one. The court's priority is to ensure the children (where there are any) are housed or re-housed properly and, in the past, courts often ordered the house not to be sold until the children finished schooling. These types of orders (in legal jargon *Mesher Orders*) are now becoming less popular, largely due to the problems which ensued with past Mesher orders, when the time finally came to sell. These could arise both in practical terms as the ex-wife had settled very comfortably into the former family home, and in terms of capital taxes (see below).

Once a proportionate division has been determined, the sale can be postponed until other events occur, for example: the remarriage of the wife or her permanent co-habitation with another person (normally taken to be at least six months); a specific date; if the wife decides to sell (for example, to move to another part of the country). Where there is sufficient cash available, and the children will not be greatly disturbed by a move, the court will usually order a sale. If the home is held in joint names, the assumption that the net proceeds of sale (after deduction of the mortgage, estate agent's commission and conveyancing costs) should be divided equally may be changed by circumstances. Again, if the wife is looking after the children she will need a bigger property to live in and is less likely to be able to afford large mortgage repayments. In many cases, an ex-wife with children might expect to receive the lion's share of the net proceeds, perhaps even an outright transfer.

Where there are no children, and the marriage has been short and both parties are able to work, if the house is jointly owned the net proceeds will probably be divided equally. Where the home is in the husband's sole name and the marriage has been short, the amount an ex-wife will be allocated depends on the length of the marriage, her contribution to the family (not just in financial terms) the earning power of both partners and so on. As each individual's case is exactly that – individual – you need to get legal advice on what would be a proper settlement in your special case.

CONTENTS OF THE HOME

Division of the household contents has already been discussed (see page 11). Unless your home is chock-full of valuable antiques, legal battles over the splitting up of the contents are not cost effective: it is sensible to give up items of sentimental value rather than pay your solicitor three times what they are actually worth.

Contents should be divided according to greatest need (who needs the fridge more?). Try to agree a schedule of items which are agreed and if there is anything left over, put those items on a second schedule. One method of dividing up contentious items is to list them, allocate them by way of odd and even numbers (for example, odd items to the husband, evens to the wife), then throwing the dice or a coin to decide who takes odds or evens to prevent cheating. Otherwise, you could consider buying some items from each other.

Guidelines used by the court are as follows:

1. Property owned by either spouse before the marriage remains his or hers.
2. Property bought with either partner's own money remains his or hers.
3. Wedding presents and gifts follow the partner whose friends or relations made the gift.
4. Items bought from joint monies or for the family are generally viewed as joint assets.

TAX IMPLICATIONS

Stamp Duty

Transfers of property over the value of £30,000 are normally subject to 1 per cent stamp duty. However, a transfer of property between husband and wife taking place after 26 March 1985, which forms part of a court order in divorce or judicial separation proceedings or part of a settlement, attracts duty of just 50p.

Mortgage Interest Relief

Any home owner is entitled to basic rate tax relief on the interest payable on a loan or loans up to £30,000 taken out to purchase or improve structurally a home. Tax relief is given at source usually under the MIRAS scheme (mortgage interest relief at source).

Once you have separated, if you purchase your own separate properties you will *each* be entitled to interest relief on mortgages up to £30,000. For mortgages taken out after 1 August 1988, mortgage interest relief attaches to the property not to the borrowers as previously.

If a husband transfers the property into his ex-wife's sole name but still pays the mortgage, those payments could be specified as maintenance payments to the ex-wife by way of a court order. This enables his wife to claim tax relief on mortgage payments. The husband should then be able to take out his own mortgage and get tax relief on that. Most building societies and banks are unwilling to grant a loan on a second property if the intended borrower is still *actually* paying the mortgage repayments (payment of maintenance does not count per se) or is responsible for the repayments. However if a husband remains guarantor for his ex-wife's mortgage repayments, as she is primarily responsible to her mortgagee, the husband should be able to get a mortgage to enable him to purchase a second property.

Capital Taxes

There were two types of capital taxes pre 1986 – capital gains tax (CGT) and capital transfer tax (CTT). CTT was abolished in the 1986 Finance Act on lifetime gifts and was replaced by

Inheritance Tax (IT) which applies to bequests on death or made just before death.

CGT is thus the only capital tax which need normally concern you on separation. It is a tax chargeable on profits made when you sell an investment or property at a higher price than you paid for it. If you have made losses, you can set these off against the gains and reduce the tax. Individuals have an annual exemption for gains up to a certain limit.

Changes made in the Finance Act 1988

For disposals made on or after 6 April 1988 there will be rebasing to 1982 so that only gains or losses accrued since 1982 will be brought into account. This removes liability on inflationary capital gains. In addition, gains are chargeable to CGT at the rates that would apply if they were at the top slice of income.

Effectively, CGT has been altered so that it dovetails with income tax rates and the annual exemption has been lowered.

Up to 5 April 1988, this annual exemption was higher for individuals (£6,600 per annum) and CGT was charged at only 30 per cent.

Principal Private Residence Exemption

You do not have to pay CGT on the gains realized on the sale of your home as long as it is your principal private place of residence. However, this can cause problems if the house is sold some time after you separate. The Inland Revenue will not normally charge CGT on transfers of assets between husband and wife (for example, stocks and shares or antiques) right up to the end of the tax year in which they separate, so if you move quickly you can avoid CGT. After separation, the husband and wife should each get their own annual exemption for CGT (a married couple only have one exemption between them).

If you have to realize or transfer some shares to make up a lump sum payment to your spouse, you must take into account an estimate (done professionally if necessary) of the capital gains tax you will have to pay and this will be brought into account by the court in its calculations.

Even after the budget of 1988, where a husband and wife are living together, they only have one annual exemption. The difference will be that each spouse, from April 1990, will be responsible for CGT divided in proportion to his or her respective capital gains.

Co-habitees each have an annual exemption for CGT but transfer of assets other than the home will attract CGT in the usual way.

Financial Proceedings: the Position for Co-Habitees

While no one has as yet uncovered statistics for the numbers of people living together throughout the UK, it is widely accepted that more people than ever before are choosing to co-habit rather than marry. Until the Finance Act 1988 took effect, cohabitation had significant tax advantages. Some of the benefits were as follows (changes made by the 1988 Finance Act in brackets):

1. Each partner could claim tax relief on a mortgage of up to £30,000 – even if the two mortgages were on one home and if the property was bought before 1 August 1988 (resulting in a tax saving then of about £17 per week). (*Change*: for all house purchases made after 1 August 1988, mortgage interest relief is available only on the first £30,000 of the loan.)

2. If each partner owned a property, one partner could claim the CGT principal private residence exemption (see previous page for one and the other for the second home by way of election. (*Change*: none)

3. While both partners only received the single person's tax-free allowance (as opposed to a married man's higher allowance) investment income received by the woman co-habitee would have been taxed as her own and she could use her tax allowance against all income received

(as opposed to a married woman who only got an allowance against her earned income). (*Change*: from 6 April 1990, married women will be taxed independently and will be able to offset all income against their tax allowance.)

4. If there were children, the single parent's Additional Personal Allowance (APA) was payable and by claiming for one child each, a co-habiting couple could get two allowances. (*Change*: from 6 April 1989 an unmarried couple living together can claim no more than one APA between them.)

5. The partner who had a higher income could make out a deed of covenant to pay income to the poorer partner to make full use of tax allowances, which would have resulted in a welcome tax refund. (*Change*: for all covenanted payments made to individuals after 15 March 1988, the payer will no longer qualify for the relief but the recipient will be exempt from them on the monies received.)

Post-Separation

Any financial advantages there may have been are stripped away after a separation. A female co-habitee then usually finds herself in a much worse financial position than her married sister. Rights available to women in divorce proceedings are largely taken away from women co-habitees, however long they have lived with their partners. They can claim no maintenance for themselves, only for the children under the affiliation proceedings or its latter-day equivalent under the Family Law Reform Act 1987 (see page 79). Any division of property will depend on each partner's ability to prove he or she actually owns part or all of it. However inequitable, a woman with no children may find herself with only personal belongings and no home to go to.

The law, while offering little support to ex-cohabiting women, makes their position worse because of the confusion inherent in it. Family law is based on marriage (and divorce). Little legislation has ever been passed to clarify the position between ex-cohabitees save on the specific subjects of illegitimacy and domestic violence. You are thus faced with old 'equitable' doctrines resurrected by Lord Denning in his pioneering work in cases heard in the 1960s and 1970s. This batch of cases is often referred to by lawyers as the 'mistress cases'. Case law is none the less conflicting and the legal position is a potential minefield. You must seek expert legal advice before deciding what to do.

PROPERTY OWNERSHIP

The main question to ask, which is almost always conclusive, is whose name appears on the title deeds of the property. If you don't know for sure you must first ascertain whether the property is registered or unregistered (see page 7 for how to ascertain the ownership).

Ownership of the property follows the name on the title deeds, unless you and your ex-partner have specifically agreed to the contrary. If it is just your ex-partner's name, you have problems.

If you own the property (usually the house) jointly, the law presumes you own it on a 50/50 basis unless there is definite (usually written) evidence to show otherwise. Co-habiting couples when buying property together should always establish at the beginning the percentage share in it each one has. For example, if only one partner put in capital to enable the couple to buy and the house is placed in joint names, if the couple later decide to separate, it would be reasonable to assume that the partner who came up with the cash should get his or her money back and the balance of the net sale proceeds be divided equally. But the law is not clear. The partner without cash could argue later that his/her once richer ex-partner intended the whole net proceeds of sale to be divided equally. If you envisage that sort of fight, the only winners will be the lawyers, so sort it out in advance if you can. One method can be to place a letter with the title deeds saying how you both want the money to be divided later, if you separate and have to sell the house.

However, this advice may come too late. What do you do if you did not make specific provision at the time?

If you, as a joint owner, feel that a 50/50 division is inequitable or, as a non-owner, feel that you do have some proprietal interest, you will have to show that the property is held *on trust* and that you and your partner had intended you to have a greater share or just a share of the property. This can be demonstrated by your having contributed to the purchase price or to any structural improvements to the property or having made mortgage repayments or possibly having paid other bills to free your partner's income to pay the mortgage. Much will also depend on the length of time you have lived together in the property. If, for example, a man moved into his girlfriend's flat for a few months, paying half the housekeeping but none of the other bills, from a common-sense viewpoint it is clear that he should have no property interest. At the other end of the scale is an ex-cohabitant who has contributed quite substantially to the property which none the less has remained in her ex-partner's sole name. What you have to establish is a *property right* – no easy matter.

If you have not got a letter or other written evidence to prove your intentions, you should search to see if there are any other documents which you can produce to substantiate your claim (for example, look at letters of instruction to your solicitor when you purchased, the mortgage application, bank accounts and so on).

If your ex-partner will not agree on a division or on a sale of the property, you are faced with the prospect of an application to the Chancery Division of the High Court (immortalized in Charles Dickens's novel *Bleak House*). Rather than get bogged down in this archaic and cumbersome Division, you can apply to transfer the case to the Family Division of the court for it to hear your application. Even the Family Division, normally flexible in its approach, has to follow enshrined equitable doctrines which were first developed in the Chancery Division. You must prepare yourself for a long and costly fight.

OTHER PROPERTY

This again depends on whose name appears as the owner. Joint accounts should be divided equally. Accounts in one partner's sole name usually belong to him or her even if you have contributed to the account. With regard to home contents, refer to the list on page 124 which applies to co-habiting couples too. (Change 'spouse' to 'partner' and 'marriage' to 'relationship'.) A more tricky question involves property in one partner's sole name (for example, a car) which was purchased from joint monies. You have a case here for arguing you own part of that asset, but do check with your solicitor first.

MAINTENANCE

Unmarried couples have no obligation to maintain one another, neither during the relationship itself nor afterwards. If you have any children, both of you are responsible for maintaining them.

12 Scotland

Scottish law finds its origins in a Roman law system which in many ways presents a more cohesive, common-sense approach to family law. While the laws of England and Wales and Scotland respectively have been changed so that they resemble each other more closely, there are still divergences, particularly in the systems and practice.

Divorce – the Procedure

The Scottish equivalents of the divorce county courts and high court are the sheriff courts and court of session in Edinburgh.

In Scotland there is no waiting period of one year after you marry before you can divorce – you can go straight from the church to the court if you so wish. The spouse who asks for a divorce is called a Pursuer, the other partner is called a Defender. Unlike in England and Wales, there is only one decree of divorce and no differentiation is made between decree nisi and decree absolute. However, a Scottish decree can be appealed against within twenty-one days of being granted.

The grounds for divorce are the same. The procedure for getting that divorce can be simpler. There is a fast procedure for getting a divorce where there are no children or no children under sixteen and no financial claims are being made; and the petition is based on either two years' separation by consent or five years' separation. Otherwise, the procedure is a little more involved than its English counterpart. Proceedings for divorce are commenced by the pursuer filing in court a summons, which is then served on the defender. The defender must tell the court whether he/she will consent to the divorce. If not, the divorce becomes defended and a full hearing takes place. If consent is forthcoming, the pursuer prepares and files an affidavit dealing with the arrangements for the children and finances. This is then sent to the court. If there are children, the pursuer must also enlist the services of another witness (normally a near relative or neighbour) who swears an affidavit dealing with the arrangements for them. A judge will examine the affidavits and, if satisfactory, he/she will pronounce the decree without the necessity of the parents' attendance at court. The divorce can then be processed by paperwork only with neither party having to attend.

Scottish Common Law Marriage

North of the border, common law marriage was never abolished as it was in England over two hundred years ago. Where a couple have lived together in a long-lasting and stable relationship, they can be regarded as married 'by co-habitation and repute'. If you have put in the necessary time and commitment you could have the benefit of the same remedies through divorce proceedings rather than relying on a strict property division.

Financial Proceedings

If there is a dispute, either the pursuer or defender must ask for a capital payment *before* the decree is granted. After that, it will be too late.

The terminology is different. Maintenance in Scotland is termed *periodical allowance*: for children, *aliment*. Aliment can be paid under a formula called *the huggins*. This is a form of words included in the court order to the effect that payments will be made to the mother as curator (trustee) for the child.

Tax relief was available both on periodical allowances and under the huggins formula as above before the Finance Act

1988. For orders made after 30 June 1988, 'maintenance' will be taxable in the hands of the payer but not the payee.

Enforcement of maintenance arrears in Scotland differs slightly. A wife whose ex-husband has failed to comply with an order for maintenance can ask the sheriff officer to assist, who then endeavours to collect money on her behalf. His remedies are stronger – he can have the husband's wages frozen completely.

Division of capital and the matrimonial home largely follow the principles already discussed, although the clean break legislation came slightly later in Scotland. The Family Law (Scotland) Act 1985 was the enabling piece of legislation.

The Scottish wife's ability to stay on in the matrimonial home, if rented, is much stronger. Under the Matrimonial Homes (Family Protection) Scotland Act 1981, a wife has the right to stay in the matrimonial home even if the husband is the legal tenant, and she cannot be evicted.

Legal Aid

Legal aid is available in Scotland for divorce proceedings. There are some minor differences. In Scotland the green form changes colour to pink; and once a full legal aid application has been approved, the certificate is backdated to when the application was made.

See 'A Guide to Legal Aid in Scotland', available from the Legal Aid Central Committee at the Law Society of Scotland (see page 174) for further details.

PART FIVE

AFTERWARDS

13 Completing the Journey: Putting Things into Effect

Having sorted out matters with your ex-partner, whether by agreement or through the courts, you now have to put into effect the moves you have decided to take. Some separated people, following the split, live in a kind of no man's land for a long time; no longer contained within the relationship but not yet quite out of it, unable to function creatively as individuals in their own right. Naturally it takes time to come to terms with loss, but at some stage you have to take a deep breath and action all of those things you have been putting off. This may involve resorting to legal remedies, as already discussed, and any or all of the following, dealt with in this chapter: moving home and/or finally dividing up the house contents, coping on your own financially and finally saying goodbye to your ex-partner (emotional completion).

Moving Home

Moving home is usually a bitter-sweet experience. However traumatic, it is a golden opportunity to mark the close of one cycle and the opening of another.

Selling (and Buying) a Home

Before you give instructions to sell, you must have arrived at an agreement with your ex-partner as to how the sale proceeds will be divided.

If the house is still jointly owned, you have to give joint sale instructions to an estate agent, so check arrangements with your partner beforehand. Otherwise you can go ahead on your own. Commission fees range from 1½ to 2½ per cent plus VAT or even more in 'exclusive' areas. The fee will be less if you give instructions for a sole agency. Beware agreeing any sole agency wherever possible, otherwise, if you are forced to instruct other agents who find you a purchaser, you may find yourself paying two lots of commission on completion of the sale. If you want to sell quickly, instruct several agents jointly – at least three. The estate agents may not like the arrangement, but you tap into a larger market and force the agents to compete with each other to get the sale, even if the fees you pay are somewhat higher.

Whenever you can, you should try to tie up your sale and intended purchase so that they happen on the same date. Being left homeless or having two properties on your hands are equally unattractive scenarios. Look for your future home to buy, if not in advance, at least at the same time that your existing home is on the market. You should identify areas that you wish to live in and then place yourself on the mailing lists of local estate agents specifying your requirements in terms of size and price.

Checklists

Moving home clocks up almost as many points on a stress scale as the separation itself. The tension is often attributable not only to the strain of leaving the emotional security of the home base behind but also to the logistical burden of organization required. The checklists which follow give an outline of what you have to do to make your move go smoothly.

Selling

- Inform your solicitor you intend to sell so that draft contracts can be prepared and a local authority search put in hand (this will save time later).
- Advertise yourself or instruct estate agents and await potential buyers.

- Receive offer; decide what items should be included in the sale (e.g. carpets, curtains, cooker).
- Confirm sale particulars with your solicitor who will then handle the legal work with your purchaser's solicitor including answering enquiries.
- Sign and exchange contracts and fix a date for completion through your solicitor (normally one month later).
- Complete the sale, pay off any costs and fees and divide the balance if necessary.

Buying

- Inquire about competitive interest rates from different building societies or banks and approach one or two in principle.
- Find a suitable property through estate agents or through adverts in (local or even national) newspapers.
- Make a 'subject to contract' offer to the vendors; agree which items (e.g. carpets, curtains, kitchen fixtures) are included in the sale.
- Instruct your solicitor who will then make the necessary inquiries and carry out searches on your behalf.
- Arrange your mortgage and survey if necessary. Building societies tend to have two types of surveys; one just a valuation the other involving a limited property survey. If you want a full structural survey you should instruct an independent surveyor.
- Sign your contract and pay a deposit (usually 10 per cent) to your solicitor who then exchanges contracts to synchronize with your sale if appropriate.
- Make removal or moving arrangements.
- Complete the purchase; find out in advance where the keys will be.

Moving

- Contact the schools that your children will attend and enrol them; advise the heads of their present schools that they will be leaving.

- Change doctors.
- Arrange with your vendor to let you into the house to measure up and arrange for specialist firms to inspect and report if appropriate (e.g. damp-proofing or timber treatment).
- Get removal estimates from different firms or arrange for van hire (and rope in friends). Check that the goods are insured in transit.
- Inform local authority and utility companies (gas, electricity, telephone, water board) you will be moving and on what date and arrange for meter readings at your old address and connections at your new address. You may be entitled to refunds for rates from the local authority; arrange for bills for utilities to be sent to your new address.
- Inform the bank of your change of address; cancel old standing orders and make out fresh mandates where appropriate.
- Likewise inform credit card companies, magazines, periodicals, etc.
- Cancel newspapers and milk.
- Arrange insurance cover for house contents (and buildings if you are buying a freehold property).
- Tell your relatives, friends and employer about your change of address and telephone number where relevant.
- Pack up your belongings and contents, labelling the boxes clearly where you want them to go and keep easily to hand a kettle, cups and refreshments to ease the burden.

Rented Accommodation

PRIVATE

If you are moving from privately rented accommodation, try not to move to accommodation which offers you a less secure position than you have already. If you are a statutory tenant (check with your solicitor if in any doubt), a landlord cannot evict you without very good reason, and in many circumstances he or she will have to offer you reasonable alternative accommodation. In addition, you may have the right to transfer your tenancy to another member of your family, so think carefully before you move.

Pressures on privately rented accommodation are high, particularly in cities. You may find yourself offered a 'company let' or 'holiday let'. Both of these are designed to get around the Rent Acts which give rights to tenants. Another problem is that of existing tenants seeking 'key money'; a capital payment for the transfer of the tenancy. Such payments are illegal but none the less are common when the property you want to rent is sought after. Make sure such tenants have the right to transfer the tenancy and in all cases take advice before moving.

HOUSING ASSOCIATIONS

If your council waiting list stretches into infinity (or is even closed as in some London boroughs), it is worth considering housing associations. Often based on a co-operative structure, most aim to supply specific housing needs, for example for single parents, or for those who have been homeless for six months. Public libraries usually hold several housing association directories, or you can inquire at your local town hall for information.

COUNCIL HOUSING

Again, housing pressures on many local authorities mean that the system is reaching breaking point. If your local authority is under pressure, think about applying for a transfer (either within your area or moving to another). You will need to apply to the local housing department, explaining your reasons for wanting to transfer and specifying what sort of accommodation you want. Ask to be placed on the transfer list. If you are offered a property, you may only have the right of up to two refusals if you think the property on offer is not suitable. If you decide to accept, ask the council if they will meet or contribute towards any repairs or redecoration you feel are necessary.

Coping on Your Own Financially

In the preceding chapters, we have concentrated on a division of income and capital – if there was any in the first place. However, all too often after divorce or separation what little existing capital there was has been used up and you are forced to use your ingenuity and perseverance to maximize the cash available to you. See whether you are entitled to any benefits as described below to augment your income.

State Benefits

There was a massive re-organization of state benefits in 1987–8 and an entirely new system of benefits was introduced, taking effect from 11 April 1988. You will have to check with your local DHSS office for the benefits which may be applicable to you. In outline, you may be able to claim one or more of the following.

FAMILY CREDIT

This is a new social security benefit that replaced family income supplement. There is a basic amount of 'adult credit' payable, together with amounts for dependent children (payable on an increasing scale, depending on age). There are, however, capital limits, and if you have savings above a certain level (in 1988: £6,000), you will not be entitled to claim family credit benefit. If you have savings, but not as much as the cut-off figure, your benefit may be reduced.

CHILD BENEFIT

While the abolition of child benefit has been broached by the government recently, at present everyone who has a child under sixteen or between sixteen and eighteen and still in full-time school education, is entitled to claim a fixed weekly amount of child benefit. In addition, single parents (for a first or only child) can claim a further, smaller weekly amount known as one-parent benefit.

INCOME SUPPORT

Replacing supplementary benefit, this is a social security benefit to help people who do not have enough cash to live on. Again, the limits within which you can qualify are very strict and vary according to your age if you are younger than twenty-five. A couple claiming income support will receive less than two individual claimants claiming separately.

SPECIAL NEEDS

In addition, you may be entitled to different premiums – extra weekly amounts for people with special needs. In 1988, special needs payments were as follows. If you have at least one child you qualify for the *Family Premium*. If you have a child who is getting *Attendance Allowance* or *Mobility Allowance* who is registered blind, you qualify for the *Disabled Child's Premium* (£6.15). If you are bringing up one or more children on their own you qualify for the *Lone Parent Premium* (£3.70).

In certain circumstances, you can apply for additional premiums (for example Disability Premium or Severe Disability Premium, Pensioner Premium or Higher Pensioner Premium).

HOUSING BENEFIT

This is a local-authority-administered government scheme to assist people on low incomes towards payment of rent and rates.

From April 1988 onwards, even if you are on a very low income, you will be held responsible for your rates (or the latter-day equivalent: the poll tax). You must make inquiries at your local town hall to find out what amounts you are likely to pay and what assistance you can claim towards payment.

The housing benefit payments are paid in a similar way to the payments made under income support (detailed above).

In certain special cases, you may be able to claim other benefits from your DHSS for example: Attendance Allowance; Guardian's Allowance; Invalid Care Allowance.

If you wish for further information, contact your local Citizens' Advice Bureau for help.

Protecting Your Future

Insurance, pensions and wills constitute three important areas which you ignore at your peril. Once you have sorted out the short-term division of your assets, you should plan for the longer term.

INSURANCE

Check that your insurance cover post-separation is adequate for your change in circumstances. Insurance policies that you might consider taking out, if you do not already have suitable protection, are as follows:

Buildings insurance: insurance against the destruction or damage of your property (e.g. by fire) for privately owned freehold property. If you own a leasehold property your landlord should arrange this for you upon payment of the proportional premium (related to the rebuilding cost of the whole property) by way of service charge.

Contents insurance: to protect against the loss of, theft of or damage to your belongings.

Car insurance: either 'third party, fire and theft' (the statutory minimum) or 'comprehensive' (providing you with full cover in the event of an accident).

Life insurance: either 'without profits' for payment only on death or 'with profits' (sometimes called an endowment policy) which provides you with a tax-free lump sum benefit at the end of its term if you pay all the premiums.

Health insurance: private health plan to cover medical

expenses and/or insurance by the *payee* against the *payer* of maintenance getting sick.

Insurance cover against a change in the amount of maintenance due: it is now possible to insure someone else's life and provide cover against cessation of maintenance due to unforeseen circumstances, for example, the death of the payer or his incapacity to pay due to illness or bankruptcy.

Check with your solicitor or insurance broker which policies you need to take out, balanced by what resources you have to pay the premiums (don't fall prey to charming insurance salesmen and take out more policies than you can afford).

PENSION POLICIES

Private Pensions

You and/or your partner may be beneficiaries of private pension schemes, either run by an employer or run as a self-employed scheme. There are usually two types of benefit in occupational pensions: *death in service*, where a widow should get an income before her late husband's anticipated date of retirement, together with a lump sum (often three times the last annual salary) together with a pension thereafter; and *retirement pensions*, where, if the employee dies after retirement, his widow will get a pension for her remaining years.

Pension rights are often a valuable asset but are difficult to assess in terms of immediate benefit, unless a partner is on the point of retirement. This is because they depend upon future events, death and retirement. Accordingly, a spouse's potential claim to be compensated for the loss of this benefit is difficult to quantify. Assuming men to be the main beneficiaries of pension schemes, their ex-wives under the age of forty are unlikely to receive much by way of a compensatory lump sum. Above that age, where the marriage has been long-lasting, pension rights should be taken into account in divorce proceedings and will usually strengthen an ex-wife's claim for a larger lump sum.

If you have been co-habiting, you have no right to your

ex-partner's pension, even though you may have been nominated as a beneficiary in the event of his or her death.

Most company pension schemes are run by trustees who have the ultimate responsibility for managing the pension funds and determining who should receive benefits. Employees protected by such schemes can nominate as beneficiary whoever they wish, if they are divorced or single. Some people still nominate their ex-spouses as beneficiaries post-separation, but it goes without saying that there can be a change of mind at any time.

Divorce and pensions are not natural bed-fellows. Your life after retirement may be considerably poorer in prospect post-separation. So, if you have not had the opportunity on separation to obtain a share of your ex-partner's pension plans, take advice about starting afresh with your own scheme.

State Pensions and National Insurance

Your entitlement to a state pension depends on either paying or being credited as having paid National Insurance contributions. As an employee, National Insurance contributions are automatically deducted from your wage packet. Self-employed people pay a fixed monthly amount together with a percentage of their profits. As a married woman, you are credited with notional annual payments if your husband has been employed, but only during the period of the marriage.

After divorce, as an ex-wife, you can start making contributions yourself or, if you are registered as unemployed, you will be given credited contributions. To qualify for a full state pension, you need to have paid National Insurance contributions for about nine-tenths of your notional working life. Otherwise, you may only be entitled to a reduced state pension.

For that period, you can make your ex-husband's or ex-wife's contributions count towards your pension if his or her record for payment exceeds your own but this option is not open to you if you re-marry before retirement age.

In all cases, particularly if you intend to rely on your

ex-partner's contributions, ensure you make contact with the DHSS before your planned retirement date. The department should contact you four months in advance of that date. If they have not done so three months in advance – call them.

WILLS

People often seem to think that if they make a will, they are more likely to die. Such thinking is superstitious nonsense and you must take time to think about what should happen to your money and possessions and to your children in the event of your death.

Divorce affects inheritance under your will although it does not automatically revoke a will. An ex-spouse cannot benefit under a will unless he or she has been named as the residuary beneficiary (the person who gets the net estate, once debts and fees have been paid off and specific bequests of items or sums of money paid out) and cannot act as an executor (the person who administers or manages the estate). If you have not made a will, your ex-spouse will not qualify under intestacy rules to share in your estate.

However, the position is not as simple as that. Under the Inheritance (Provision for Family and Dependants) Act 1975, broadly speaking, family members or persons financially dependent on you prior to your death may be able to make a claim against your estate. It is thus prudent to make a will setting out your testamentary intentions and leave a letter with the original will to explain why you do not want your ex-partner to receive any share (if this is the case). In divorce proceedings you can cover yourself fully by getting a specific order from the court that your ex-spouse will not be entitled on your death to any share of your estate.

If you have children, you can make specific provision in a will to say whom you would like to appoint as a guardian or guardians after your death. This may be particularly apposite where you have a new partner and your offspring's other natural parent is showing little interest in them. Your declaration will not guarantee the person nominated being appointed as a guardian but will have persuasive force before a court as long as your appointee can show that his/her appointment is in the children's best interests.

A will, unlike divorce proceedings, is inexpensive – about £40 or so from your solicitor or even free if you qualify under a green form (see page 95). It is advisable to see a solicitor if you have complex intentions. Alternatively, you can get a sample will form from some stationers. If you do insist on having a do-it-yourself will, be careful to read and follow the instructions otherwise the whole document may be invalid.

Remember also that if you re-marry, a will will be automatically revoked unless it was prepared specifically with that marriage in mind.

A will is not affected by a decree of divorce in Scotland or Northern Ireland.

Emotional Completion

References have been made throughout this book to the state of 'psychological marriage', where one ex-partner refuses to give up the relationship. It may be that, unfortunately, your ex-partner is still psychologically married to you. Your best tactic in such circumstances is to explain kindly but clearly that your time together is over. Eventually he or she may listen and start afresh on a new cycle of life. If your ex-partner refuses to listen to you, recognize that this is his or her own choice. You can only be responsible for your own life.

It may, however, be you that is in this limbo state, not yet daring to accept that the old partnership is over because it means, for one thing, that you have to take responsibility for yourself in the future. Having lived a life so far dependent on another, it is of course daunting to think of carving out an independent life for yourself in the future; daunting but none the less challenging. A life of dependency can submerge your own personality under that of another. You now have the opportunity to create a fully rounded existence for the future.

It all takes time. But one of the essential stages of the journey towards fuller self-discovery is to say goodbye to a period of your life which has now ended. For divorcing couples, this can be the time of decree nisi if they attend together at court and hear a judge pronounce the words formally dissolving the marriage; or it can be the time when the decree absolute certificate arrives on the doorstep. For others, the moment when you know, deep within yourself, that it is all over, can come earlier or later. Most of us can point to a specific date which marked the turning point.

Inasmuch as a new relationship sometimes needs or is enhanced by a ritual (for example, the wedding ceremony or being carried over the threshold of a new home or an informal exchange of promises) to mark its beginning, so its natural end can be made clearer by a form of ceremony. If you find yourself unwilling to forget, let alone forgive, explore whether you and your ex-partner can come together for one last time, over dinner or just for an hour or so at a private meeting place, to say to each other anything that you have been wanting to but have been unable to say so far and, most importantly, to say goodbye to that chapter of your life. If your ex-partner will not co-operate, you could set up for yourself some kind of ritual or ceremony, perhaps writing down your relationship history and then burning the paper to symbolize your freedom from that relationship. Remember the good parts as well as the bad, and then assign this time to your past.

Some conciliation agencies, or other agencies working with couples in distress, have worked out their own form of ritual. One such ceremony frequently takes place in the offices of a senior divorce court welfare officer in Birmingham. Mrs Sheila Davis, who introduced the scheme, asks couples to stand in her office while she takes them by the hands, and tells them to bid farewell along the following lines: 'Goodbye. Thank you for the good times in our marriage. I wish you luck in your new life. Our relationship will continue as mother and father of our children, but not as husband and wife.'

Mrs Davis, who was herself divorced and has since remarried, introduced this scheme to help people separate emotionally. She has been reported as saying that the language used by each of the couples can be 'rather blunt, but I like people to use their own words. Sometimes they simply say: "Sod off, and thanks for all you did."'

Acceptance of the past and forgiveness of yourself and your partner are the keys to the ending of this particular chapter and the opening of the doors to your new life.

14 Beginning Your New Life

There comes a moment when you reach the end of your journey of separation. It comes at different times for us all but it is instantly recognizable when it comes. The moment is the point when you wake up and feel alive instead of deadened, when your own sorrow recedes and you begin again to listen to the birds singing and children laughing in the street. You may feel the urge to take up a hobby or have a holiday or just go for a walk. You may now have more time to enjoy your friends. If you have time to spare and would like to widen your circle, take up that hobby or activity you always yearned after, there is nothing stopping you now, whether it be hang-gliding, walking in the Himalayas, flower-arranging or gardening. Join a club or group to meet new people with similar interests. Rebuild your life the way you want it to look; there is nothing to stop you but yourself.

Once you have reached this important stage, you are likely to view your life through new eyes. You have gone through a catharsis and your perceptions and your beliefs may have been altered. You may find that in leaving your old self behind there are old friends whom you are no longer close to. Some friends are unable to acknowledge that we have changed as they themselves are resistant to change. They complain we are different and are anxious to push us back into the pattern from which we have just broken out. If your old friends make you feel uncomfortable, however much you try to explain, you may have to break with them. In the best interests of your true self, be firm and break away – new friendships will be soon forged to take their place.

Having emerged from your past relationship, it is immediately tempting to throw yourself into a new one – to forget the past by beginning an exciting bond with someone else. However, beware new relationships struck up while the drama of the old is still unfinished. Relationships forged in the heat of a separation, to escape the pain of the present or on the rebound, are unlikely to live up to expectations. Without giving yourself time and space to rediscover who you are, you are likely to want to rush headlong into a new relationship without considering whether it is really right for you. You may have unrealistic hopes that this one will work, leading you to idealize the new person.

Placing someone on a pedestal is not the best way to go about starting a new relationship. It may work but the odds are against it. Resist, if you can, the urge to get involved again too quickly. Let some time elapse before starting any new, intimate relationship. Allow those relationships to start gradually, building up slowly so that the foundations you create are solid and deep. Find out if you *like* someone first before committing yourself too intensely. Find out if the two of you are compatible and make a friend of your potential lover. The wait will be worthwhile. At worst, if you discover you have nothing in common, you can part early on without the added trauma of having invested yourself heavily in another person. At best you may have the beginnings of a great relationship and have built a firm foundation on a clear knowledge of each other, warts and all. In the middle you may well have found a good friend, a gift in itself.

CELEBRATE THE ENDING

Once you do arrive at your journey's end, take a few moments to acknowledge the wonderful qualities within you which have won through. Your courage, perseverance and commitment to yourself have paid off. Recall the highs and the lows, the grief and the anger – the spectrum of emotions which have flowed through you before you have arrived at this comparative haven of acceptance. You have finally made it: congratulations! Treat yourself to an evening (or week!) of celebration – you deserve it. If others have helped you along the way, don't forget to thank them too. This can include your children who often provide a great source of emotional support. Savour the moment – an important cycle of your life has come to a close and your new life is just now beginning.

Co-habitation Contracts

People are today trying out new ways of organizing their intimate relationships. One approach, which some might consider over-cautious and unromantic, is to consider entering into a co-habitation contract. The idea is that, preferably before they begin living together, a couple discuss their intentions about the new relationship and come to an agreement over various issues. Chris Barton in his book on co-habitation contracts suggests a contract based on the following (taken from Weitzman in *Marriage Contracts*):*

(a) *statement of the purpose of the contract*, for example to create an equal relationship

(b) *legality of agreement*, for example intended to be legally binding or merely a statement of expectations

(c) *the parties*, for example statement of ages, financial disclosures and health

(d) *aims of the parties*, for example their collective and individual goals in the relationship

(e) *duration*, for example for lifetime, fixed period or until specified event

(f) *careers and employment*, for example do both want/are able to work, priorities

(g) *income and expenses*, for example how much, how to be treated, to pool or not to pool, savings

* Chris Barton *Cohabitation Contracts* (Gower).

(h) *property held at inception*, for example statement of, how to be treated

(i) *property acquired during co-habitation*, for example to be treated as community property or not, who to manage, gifts; similarly, life insurance policies and the question of making a nomination to trustees of an occupational pension fund

(j) *debts*, for example statement of what each currently owes, their attitudes to credit

(k) *living arrangements*, for example who to choose, town or country, policy as to guests

(l) *household tasks*, for example how divided

(m) *surname*, for example each to keep his or her own, one to adopt the other's, hyphenation, the position of children

(n) *sexual relations*, for example type, monogamy, rules for disclosure if not

(o) *personal behaviour*, for example smoking, hobbies, private area in house

(p) *relations with family and friends*, for example any responsibility for (such as children from previous relationship), communication of non-marital status

(q) *children*, for example to have or not to have, how to bring up

(r) *religion*

(s) *health*, for example private care, insurance

(t) *inheritance and wills*, for example what if anything, will each leave to the other

(u) *breaches of the agreement*, for example liquidated damages court proceedings, arbitration

(v) *resolving disagreements*, for example professional conciliation

(w) *changing or renewing the contract*

(x) *dissolution*, for example when, notice, support, property, custody

(y) *conversion to marriage*.

Co-habitation contracts do not need to be so involved. You will find set out in Appendix III a draft co-habitation agreement which first appeared in the *Cohabitation Handbook*.* This is a comparatively simple document although if you have more sophisticated intentions, you can draw up more complex clauses. The agreement has been included here to show what a co-habitation contract might look like in format.

It obviously places an enormous amount of pressure on a new relationship to find out what each person thinks about such a broad spectrum of issues. In the old way of behaving, couples tended to start relationships comparatively 'unconsciously' and would discover their partner's views on different subjects only piecemeal as the relationship continued. This could result in finding yourself deeply involved in a relationship with another person with whose opinions you fundamentally disagree.

The foundation of a good relationship has been said to be compromise, but when should the compromises occur – before or after? To enter into a co-habitation contract is a pioneering move. The investment at the time may reap rich rewards later in terms of knowing your partner and creating realistic expectations of your relationship. A question mark arises, however, as to whether co-habitation contracts will be held to be legally binding. The consensus of legal opinion is that they are not binding. If you are considering entering into a contract, you should take advice. Your solicitor will probably advise you to take certain additional steps to protect your position if you are co-habiting, for example, in drawing up a deed of trust concerning the home which you own, making a will and obtaining court orders concerning custody of the children, if relevant. None of these moves, obviously, could be held to be faintly romantic. However, romance should be consigned to its proper place – a candlelit dinner for two, a walk in the park or breakfast in bed – rather than used as a measure to govern the conduct of one's life as a whole. Even if you decide not to enter into a co-habitation contract, the exercise of discussing with your partner the items outlined above will illuminate the new relationship. Good Luck.

* Rights of Women (RoW) *Cohabitation Handbook* by Bottomley, Gieve, Moon and Weir (Pluto Press).

Until one is committed there is hesitancy, the chance to draw back, always ineffectiveness. Concerning all acts of initiative and creation there is one elementary truth, the ignorance of which kills countless ideas and splendid plans; that the moment one definitely commits oneself, then providence moves too. All sorts of things occur to help one that would never otherwise have occurred. A whole stream of events issues from the decision, raising in one's favour all manner of unforeseen incidents and meetings and material assistance, which no man could have dreamed would have come his way.

W. H. Murray

What ever you can do or dream, begin it. Boldness has genius, magic and power in it.
Begin it now.

Goethe

APPENDICES

APPENDIX I
Solicitors' Family Law Association Code of Practice*

The Association recommends that members and any solicitor practising family law should adopt the following code of practice.

GENERAL

1.1 The solicitor should endeavour to advise, negotiate and conduct proceedings in a manner calculated to encourage and assist the parties to reconcile their differences as quickly as may be reasonable while recognizing that the parties may need time to come to terms with their new situation, and should inform the client of the approach he intends to adopt.

1.2 The solicitor should treat his work in relation to the children as the most important of his duties. The solicitor should encourage the client to see the advantages to the family of a non-litigious approach as a way of resolving their disputes. The solicitor should explain to the client that in cases where there are children the attitude of the client to the other parent in any negotiations will affect the family as a whole and may affect the relationship of the children with the parents.

1.3 The solicitor should encourage the attitude that a family dispute is not a contest in which there is one winner and one loser, but rather a search for fair solutions. He should avoid using words or phrases that imply a dispute when no serious dispute necessarily exists, for example, 'opponent', 'win', 'lose', or 'Smith v Smith'.

* Published with permission.

1.4   Because of the involvement of personal emotions in family disputes the solicitor should where possible avoid heightening such emotions by the advice given; and by avoiding expressing opinions as to the behaviour of the other party.

1.5   The solicitor should also have regard to the impact of correspondence on the other party when writing a letter of which a copy may be sent to that party and should also consider carefully the impact of correspondence on his own client before sending copies of letters to the client.

1.6   The solicitor should aim to avoid or dispel suspicion or mistrust between parties, by encouraging at an early stage where possible, full, frank and clear disclosure of information and openness in dealings.

1.7   The solicitor should aim to achieve settlement of difference as quickly as may be reasonable whilst recognizing that the parties may need time to come to terms with their new situation.

RELATIONSHIP WITH CLIENT

2.1   As a rule the solicitor should explain to the client at the outset the terms of his retainer and take care to ensure that the client is fully aware of the impact of costs on any chosen course of action. The solicitor should thereafter at all stages have regard to the cost of negotiations and proceedings.

2.2   Where appropriate, the solicitor must advise the client of his right to apply for Legal Aid. He should bear in mind and explain the impact of costs where the client or the other party is in receipt of Legal Aid, and the particular effect of the statutory charge.

2.3   The solicitor should create and maintain a relationship with his client of a kind which will preserve fully his independent judgement and avoid becoming so involved in the case that his own personal emotions may cloud his judgement.

2.4   Whilst recognizing the need to advise firmly and guide the client the solicitor should ensure that where the decision is properly that of the client, it is taken by the client and that its consequences are fully understood, both as to its effect on any children involved and financially.

DEALINGS WITH OTHER SOLICITORS

3.1   The solicitor should in all dealings with the other solicitor show courtesy and where possible endeavour to create and maintain a friendly relationship.

3.2   The solicitor should seek wherever possible to foster in his own client a trust in the other party's solicitor, so tending to reduce distrust and suspicion between the parties.

3.3   The solicitor should in financial negotiations make use of without prejudice discussions, that is to say discussions involving conditional offers and conditional admissions that are withdrawn and not disclosed to the Court in the event of those negotiations failing. The solicitor should be mindful that an unrealistic offer may be counter-productive and delay settlement.

DEALINGS WITH THE OTHER PARTY IN PERSON

4.1   In dealings with another party who is not legally represented the solicitor should take particular care to be courteous and restrained. Especial care should be taken to express letters and other communications clearly, avoiding technical language where it is not readily understandable to the layman or might be misunderstood.

4.2   Wherever proceedings are taken or negotiations conducted that may adversely affect the other party's interests, the other party should, in the interests of both parties, be advised to consult a solicitor.

PETITIONS AND PROCEEDINGS

5.1   The solicitor should avoid allegations or procedures which may cause or increase ill-will between the parties without producing any benefit for the client.

5.2 Before instituting proceedings which make allegations about the other party's conduct, the solicitor should consider whether the other party or his solicitor should be consulted in advance as to the particulars to be alleged or the grounds to be relied on.

5.3 Where the purpose of taking a particular step in proceedings may be misunderstood the solicitor should consider explaining it in advance to the other party or his solicitors.

CHILDREN

6.1 The solicitor should, in advising, negotiating and conducting proceedings, assist both his client and the other parent to regard the welfare of the child as the first and paramount consideration.

6.2 The solicitor should aim to promote co-operation between parents in decisions concerning the child, both by formal arrangements (such as orders for joint custody), by practical arrangements (such as shared involvement in school events) and by consultation on important questions.

6.3 The solicitor must keep in mind that the interests of the child do not necessarily coincide with the interests of either parent, and that occasionally the child should be separately represented. In such cases his duty is to bring the matter to the attention of the Court.

6.4 The solicitor should take care to keep separate issues of custody and access on the one hand and money on the other. It is often helpful to deal with these two topics in separate letters.

6.5 'Kidnapping' of children both results from and creates exceptional fear, bitterness and desperation in the parents. The solicitor should therefore take what steps he can to prevent the kidnapping of a child and inform his client that he may be committing a criminal offence punishable by imprisonment.

The guidelines set out in this code cannot be absolute rules in as much as the solicitor may have to depart from them if the law or his professional obligations so require. They are a restatement of

principles, objectives and recommendations which many solicitors practising family law already seek to follow and to which
they seek to aspire in serving their clients.

September 1986

Published as part of a Green Paper on Child Custody, 1986 (see page 76).

1. The quality of the love, affection and other emotional ties existing between the child and each of the parties.
2. The nature of the emotional ties existing between the child and any person other than the parties.
3. The effect upon the child of separation from either party or from any other person with whom he has been living.
4. The capacity and disposition of each of the parties to provide for the child's emotional needs in the future including the recognition of his ties with other people.
5. The length of time the child has lived in his existing environment and the effect of any change including changes of neighbourhood, school, local activities and access to relatives and friends.
6. The capacity (bearing in mind any financial provision or property adjustment which may be ordered) and disposition of each of the parties to provide properly for the child's accommodation, hygiene, good, medical care, appropriate supervision, and companionship and otherwise for his physical needs and developments.
7. The capacity (bearing in mind any financial provision which may be ordered) and disposition of each of the parties to provide properly for the child's education and intellectual development both at home and at school.
8. The capacity and disposition of each of the parties to

provide properly for the child's social and ethical developments.

9. Where relevant the ethnic, cultural or religious background of the child and each of the parties.

10. The quality of the relationship existing or likely to exist between the child and any other member of each household and the likely effect of that member upon the capacities and dispositions of each of the parties in paragraphs 4, 6, 7, and 8 above.

11. Any risk of ill-treatment by either party or by any present or likely member of that party's household.

12. Any other special circumstances, including any particular aptitude or disability of the child.

13. The wishes and feelings of the child.

APPENDIX III
Co-habitation Contract

THIS AGREEMENT is made on the   day of
       19   BETWEEN Hilary Black of Hugo Road,
London (hereinafter called the first party)
AND Alex White of Celia Road, London (hereinafter called the
second party)
WHEREAS
The parties wish to enter into an agreement which they intend
to be legally binding upon them as to their own respective
rights during the relationship, obligations towards each other,
obligations towards any children of the relationship and
interest in any property owned jointly and separately by them
IT IS HEREBY AGREED that the parties shall live together for an
indefinite period subject to the following terms.

   1.   The parties agree that they shall have equal interests in
any premises occupied by them as the family home so that if
the legal title to such premises is vested in one party only such
title shall be held in trust for both parties in equal shares.
   2.   The parties agree that all property owned separately by
them before they began to live together shall remain their
separate property unless such property shall be occupied as the
family home, in which case the above clause applies. Any
property owned jointly by them before they began to live
together shall remain their joint property and on sale the
proceeds shall belong to them in equal shares.
   3.   The parties agree that all property acquired after they
began to live together for their joint use shall be jointly owned.

All property acquired after they began to live together for sole use of either party shall remain the property of that party.

4.   (a) The parties agree that while they both maintain separate bank accounts the monies in each bank account shall belong to the party whose name it is in.

(b) Should they decide at any time to open a joint bank account the monies in that account shall belong to both in equal shares.

(c) If at any time one of them is not in full-time paid employment because of childbirth or responsibilities of caring for children of the relationship, they shall both transfer all monies to a joint bank account but, failing this, half the monies earned by the one who is employed shall belong to the other.

5.   The parties agree that they shall be liable to meet the common expenses of the family home including all necessary outgoings such as rent and mortgage payments, rates, electricity and the expenses of maintaining the children in proportion to their respective incomes.

AND IT IS FURTHER AGREED that either party may terminate this agreement by notice of three months. Notice is to be in writing and served on the other party in person. Alternatively this agreement may be terminated without notice if the parties have ceased to live together for a period of three months. ALWAYS PROVIDED that in the event that this AGREEMENT is terminated as aforesaid THEN

6.   The parties agree that the property and chattels referred to in paragraphs 1, 2, and 3 above as joint property shall be sold and the proceeds of their sale shall be divided equally between the parties unless further agreement to the contrary is made between them, save that in the case of the family home if there are children of the relationship, the sale of the home and the joint property used in the home shall be postponed for a reasonable time and during that period the person looking after the children shall be permitted to remain there with the

children unless a further agreement to the contrary is made between the parties.

7.   The parties shall continue to maintain any children of the relationship and each shall contribute one-fifth of their respective incomes after tax in respect of each child until that child reaches the age of 16 or completes his or her full-time education.

Signed by the said HILARY BLACK   (signature)
In the presence of   (witness's signature)
Signed by the said ALEX WHITE   (signature)
In the presence of   (witness's signature)

APPENDIX IV
Legal Glossary*

Access   The right for a child to see both parents. It may consist of visits to or overnight stays by the children. A parent who does not obtain *care and control* will normally be given access. Access can be 'reasonable' (when specific terms are not laid down) or 'defined' (when the court lays down fixed times). Non-parents, e.g. grandparents, are in certain limited circumstances entitled to apply for access.

Affidavit   A statement in writing and on oath to be used as evidence in court proceedings. The person making it swears it before a SOLICITOR or court official for a fixed fee.

Affiliation Order   An order for maintenance of a child made in the MAGISTRATES' COURT which first decides whether or not a man is the child's father. May shortly be replaced by Family Law Reform Act 1987 application.

Appellant   Someone who is appealing against a decision of a court in a higher court.

Barrister   Also known as **Counsel**. Represents people in court from the MAGISTRATES' COURT up to the HOUSE OF LORDS and is consulted for opinions or advice. Can work only on the instruction of a SOLICITOR and may communicate with the client only through or in the presence of a solicitor. A barrister works from a set of chambers together with a group of barristers and is organized by one or more CLERKS. A barrister often specializes in one area of law, e.g. family law or criminal law.

* Adapted from the *Lesbian Mother's Custody Handbook* (see page 76).

Care and Control The day-to-day care of the child. This is always given to one PARTY where a court order is made.

Care Order Court order giving a local authority most of the parents' legal rights over a child.

Chambers BARRISTER's office.

In Chambers Court hearing held in private (most family cases are heard in chambers).

Clerk *see* Barrister.

Common Law Judge-made law as it has evolved over the centuries in this country, as distinct from law made by Parliament (statutory law).

Conciliation A process of resolving disputes between parents, particularly with regard to their children. Can be 'in court' or 'voluntary'. In court, a COURT WELFARE OFFICER is appointed to the case and is supposed to mediate between the parties with the assistance of the court REGISTRAR. Voluntary conciliation agencies are spreading around the country and can be used as an alternative or in addition to legal proceedings.

Conference A meeting between someone who is taking legal action and their BARRISTER. The person's SOLICITOR or representative should be present and the meeting usually takes place in the barrister's office (CHAMBERS).

Consent Order This is an agreement reached by the PARTIES and approved by the court. Approval is not always automatic. It is an order of the court and is therefore enforceable through the court.

Counsel *see* Barrister.

County Court Deals with non-criminal matters only. Divorce courts hear domestic violence cases, undefended divorces and related matters of MAINTENANCE and CUSTODY or ACCESS, guardianship (which includes custody disputes between unmarried parents) and adoption. The divorce registry in London acts as both a county and HIGH COURT.

Court of Appeal Hears appeals from the HIGH COURT and COUNTY COURT.

Court Welfare Officer A probation officer, or, in some parts of the country, a local authority social worker, who is appointed by the court to investigate in cases involving children and prepare a WELFARE REPORT or takes part in the court CONCILIATION process.

Covenant Legally binding agreement signed and witnessed.

Cross-examination Questioning of someone in court by the lawyer for the other side.

Custody This is the right to make long-term decisions affecting a child, e.g. on education, health and religion. A parent who has custody has the ultimate legal responsibility for the child, and will usually have physical CARE AND CONTROL over the child. Custody of a child can be held jointly by both parents (joint custody) or by one parent (sole custody).

Decree Absolute Court order making a divorce final.

Decree Nisi First stage of a court order for divorce.

Defined Access *see* Access.

Ex-parte An application to the court by one PARTY to proceedings without the other party having been told in advance and therefore not being represented.

Expert Witness An 'expert' witness can give his/her opinion on a subject within her/his expertise (e.g. a psychiatrist). This is an exception to the general rule that witnesses may only speak of facts which they themselves have observed and may not give their opinion on those facts.

Filing at Court Sending legal documents to the court.

Guardian ad Litem A person appointed by the court from an approved panel of social workers to act as the child's representative (sometimes together with a SOLICITOR) in care proceedings.

Hearsay Evidence Evidence of a fact not actually perceived by a witness with one of his/her own senses, but said by her/him to have been stated by another person. The general rule is that such evidence cannot be used to prove the truth of fact.

High Court The family division deals with defended divorces and can decide on related questions of MAINTENANCE, CUS-TODY and ACCESS, guardianship (includes custody disputes between unmarried parents), WARDSHIP and adoption. There are two other divisions: Queens Bench and Chancery. The chancery division is the starting place for property actions by ex-cohabitees.

House of Lords   Hears appeals from the COURT OF APPEAL but only with leave of either the court of appeal or the appeals committee of the House of Lords.

Injunction   A court order requiring someone to do, or to stop doing, something.

Interim custody/care and control   This is a temporary order in which CUSTODY and/or CARE AND CONTROL can be given to any PARTY, pending the final decision on the case.

Joint Custody   *see* Custody.

Judicial Separation   Legal separation of a married couple. The grounds are the same as for a divorce but after a judicial separation the parties remain legally married.

Judiciary   All judges, magistrates.

Law Report   A report of a court decision written up in the officially recognized reports, giving the facts of the case/ reasons for the decision. Law reports are usually written by BARRISTERS.

Law Society   Association of SOLICITORS which also administers LEGAL AID (but this power will shortly be removed by the Legal Aid Act 1988).

Leave to Appeal   Permission from the court to lodge an appeal against a decision of the court.

Legal Aid   A scheme which was run by the LAW SOCIETY and funded by public funds. It enables people whose income and capital do not exceed certain limits to have free legal advice and representation, provided they can show they have a case.

Magistrates' Court   Deals with criminal (including juvenile) and non-criminal matters. The latter include domestic violence, certain MAINTENANCE applications in which the court has power to make orders regarding CUSTODY or ACCESS, and guardianship (which includes custody disputes between unmarried parents).

Maintenance 1. Regular payments of money paid from one spouse (usually the husband) to the other spouse during or after marriage. 2. Regular payments of money for a child paid by a parent (usually the father).

Matrimonial Home House in which wife and husband live, or previously shared home of married couple.

Mediator American term for conciliator; 'holds the arena' for couples to discuss different problems.

Minor A person under the age of eighteen.

Next Friend Adult in whose name legal proceedings are taken on behalf of a child.

Official Solicitor Acts in HIGH COURT cases as the representative of a MINOR if the court decides that the minor needs independent representation.

Ouster Injunction Court order directing someone (usually a man) to leave the home.

Party Someone who is involved in a legal action.

Petitioner Person who applied to the court for a divorce.

Place of Safety Order A local authority or the police can, without notice to the parents, apply to a magistrate for an order that a juvenile be taken to a place of safety, e.g. a local authority children's home or foster home, for a maximum period of twenty-eight days.

Precedent A decision made by a previous court which can serve as a rule or pattern to be followed or considered in a subsequent case.

Reasonable Access *see* Access.

Registrar Sits in the COUNTY COURT and family division of the HIGH COURT and is appointed by the Lord Chancellor; deals with procedural issues until the trial of a matter takes place, applications for MAINTENANCE and other financial matters in divorce proceedings; deals with ACCESS to children where the principle of access is agreed and the only matter in dispute is the amount of access; presides over CONCILIATION appointments where there is a CUSTODY or access dispute.

Reported Case   A case decision which has been written up in the law reports.

Respondent (or Defendant)   Person against whom legal action is being taken.

Solicitor   Can represent people in MAGISTRATES' COURTS, COUNTY COURTS and sometimes in the crown court. Rarely represents a client in contested family matters but instead instructs a BARRISTER. A solicitor deals direct with the client and is responsible for the preparation of the case, which includes advising the client, interviewing witnesses and instructing a barrister.

Status Quo   The current state of affairs.

Statute   Law made by Parliament.

Statutory Charge   Charge made by the LAW SOCIETY for legal costs where property/money is involved (see page 94).

Supervision Order   A court order which gives the general supervision of a child to a local authority and which can last until the child is eighteen.

Testamentary Guardian   Person named in a will to have CUSTODY, CARE AND CONTROL of child/ren on a person's death.

Tort   An actionable negligent act or omission (i.e. for which you can make a civil claim in the courts).

Variation Order   Court order changing an original court order.

Ward of Court   A child who has been made a ward comes under the court's protection, i.e. all major decisions relating to the child have to be referred to the court for its approval. The person with whom the child lives has the child's CARE AND CONTROL.

Wardship Proceedings   Legal action making a child a WARD OF COURT.

Welfare Principle   This is contained in Section 1 of the Guardianship of Minors Act 1971 which states that the welfare of a child shall be regarded as the first and paramount (i.e. supreme) consideration in any proceedings relating to children.

Welfare Report   A report which may be, and frequently is, ordered by a REGISTRAR or judge in any proceedings involving children. It is prepared by a COURT WELFARE OFFICER who investigates the circumstances of any person claiming CUSTODY or ACCESS and interviews the parties and the children. The report can only be shown to the parties to the proceedings and their legal advisers.

Useful Addresses

Alcoholics Anonymous
PO Box 514
11 Redcliffe Gardens
London SW10 9BQ
Tel: 01-352 9779

Cellmark Diagnostics
Blacklands Way
Abingdon Business Park
Abingdon
Oxon OX14 1DY
Tel: 0235 28609

Central Statistical Office
Great George Street
London SW1
Tel: 01-270 6363

DHSS Leaflets Unit
PO Box 21
Stanmore
Middlesex HA7 1AY

DHSS (Public Enquiries Office)
Alexander Fleming House
Elephant and Castle
London SE1
Tel: 01-405 5522

Families Need Fathers
37 Carden Road
London SE15
Tel: 0689 54343 (central office)

Family Forum
Cambridge House
31 Camberwell Road
London SE5 0HF
Tel: 01-703 6418

Gingerbread
35 Wellington Street
London WC2
Tel: 01-240 0953

Incorporated Law Society of Northern Ireland
Bedford House
16–22 Bedford Street
Belfast BT2 7F1
Tel: 0232 246 441

Inland Revenue (Public Enquiries Room)
West Wing
Somerset House
Strand
London W C 2
Tel: 01-438 6420

Institute of Family Therapy
43 New Cavendish Street
London W 1 M 7 R G
Tel: 01-935 1651

Jewish Family Mediation Service
3 Gower Street
Bloomsbury
London W C 1
Tel: 01-636 9380

Land Charges Department
Burngate Way
Plymouth PL5 3LP
Tel: 0752 779831

Land Registry
Lincoln's Inn Fields
London WC2A 3PH
Tel: 01-405 3488

Law Society, The
113 Chancery Lane
London WC2A 1PL
Tel: 01-242 1222

Law Society of Scotland, The
PO Box 123
41–43 Drumsheugh Gardens
Edinburgh EH3 7SW
Tel: 031 226 7061

London Jewish Marriage Council
23 Ravenshurst Avenue
London NW4
Tel: 01-203 6311

Mothers Apart From Their Children (MATCH)
64 Delaware Mansions
Delaware Road
London W9

National Association of Citizens' Advice Bureaux
115 Pentonville Road
London N1
Tel: 01-833 2181

National Council for the Divorced and Separated
41 Summit Avenue
Kingsbury
London NW9

National Council for One Parent Families
255 Kentish Town Road
London NW5 2LX
Tel: 01-267 1361

National Family Conciliation Council
34 Milton Road
Swindon
Wiltshire SN1 5JH
Tel: 0793 618 486

National Foster Care Association
Francis House
Francis Street
London SW1P 1DE
Tel: 01-828 6266

National Marriage Guidance Council (Relate)
Herbert Gray College
Little Church Street
Rugby CV21 3AP
Tel: 0788 73241 or 60811

Scottish Council for Single Parents
13 Gayfield Square
Edinburgh
Tel: 031 556 3899

Solicitors Complaints Bureau
Portland House
Stag Place
London SW1
Tel: 01-834 2288

Solicitors' Family Law Association (SFLA)
Secretary: Andrew Gerry
20 Essex Street
London WC2R 3AL

Administrative inquiries to:
Mary I'Anson
SFLA
24 Croydon Road
Keston
Kent BR2 6EJ
Tel: 0689 50227

Stepfamily (National Stepfamily Association)
Room 3
Ross Street Community Centre
Ross Street
Cambridge CB1 3BS
Tel: 0223 460312

Women's Aid Federation
Tel: 01-251 6537
Crisis: 01-995 4430

Index